Lessons on Trusting Y[...]
with Confidence

THE
MARKETING
Girl

MARTINA BARLEY

BRIGHTRAY
PUBLISHING®

We help busy professionals write and publish their stories to distinguish themselves and their brands.

(407) 287-5700 | Winter Park, FL
info@BrightRay.com | www.BrightRay.com

ISBN: 978-1-956464-48-1

No part of this publication may be reproduced, stored in a retrieval system, or transmitted in any form or by any means, electronic, mechanical, photocopying, recording, or otherwise, without permission of the author. For information regarding permission, please contact the author.

Published in the United States of America.
BrightRay Publishing ® 2023

To my husband, Aaron:
You are the best bold move I've ever made.
Most of the events on these pages happened
during the years we spent apart.
Consider yourself lucky.

PRAISE FOR

"In *The Marketing Girl*, Martina masterfully delivers a message that early-stage entrepreneurs need to hear. Her 'born-out-of-spite' attitude brings forth an entertaining balance of her life stories and actionable takeaways that will both inspire you to take action and achieve success."

ALEX SHATTUCK,
Owner of Autopilot Recruiting, Alex Shattuck Insurance, Shattuck Property Group

---

"Someone recently asked me this on a panel: if I could go back in time to two to three years ago, what would I tell myself? My first reaction wasn't to tell myself anything—it was to tell Martina to write this book sooner! As a med-school dropout turned marketing executive, I found Martina's wise words hit close to home. I hope that anyone looking for inspiration, encouragement, and most importantly, some realness comes across these pages. I've had the pleasure of working with Martina in the real world, and her warm tone, brilliant humor, and undeniable charm come across with every chapter!"

CHRISTIANA YEBRA,
Owner of Currency Strategies, CMO of nVenue

"*The Marketing Girl* is a refreshingly honest and engaging take on business and personal growth. Martina's story is filled with real-life experiences, humor, and practical advice. This book is more than just a business guide; it's an invitation to live life boldly and authentically, encouraging readers to pursue their dreams on their own terms."

ANTHONY ANDERSON,
Owner of Anthony Anderson Insurance

"I've had the pleasure of knowing Martina before, during, and after she became 'the marketing girl,' and thankfully, she never stopped going when I told her she was crazy over the years. To have the opportunity to relive her journey in such great detail and to know where she came from versus who she is now completely blows me away. For the person out there wondering if you can do it, this book is for you because YOU CAN, and Martina proves that to you. If you need that extra kick in the ass, the extra push to reach your true potential, read this book and get to work!"

MARK TEMPERATO,
Owner of Dash Capital Advisors

"*The Marketing Girl* is a must-read for anyone looking for the push to make a big move. Martina is inspiring and relatable in telling her story while giving the quintessential handbook to shape your future to be exactly what you want. With the perfect mix of personal and professional insight, this book is bound to change lives!"

SHANNON O'CONNOR,
Co-Owner of Tri Beauty Company,
Owner of Stone Consulting

"BRB, going to buy another investment property, open a new investment account, and maybe get crazy and text my ex who I miss . . . Okay, seriously, I loved ALL of this. As a business owner (real estate agent) and investor, I found so much of this to be relatable, full of lessons and 'wow' moments, and a huge motivation for someone like me. I allow so much of what I want to hold me back by simply fearing the what-ifs (as most do). The vulnerability and realness of Martina and what her success story looks like is beyond inspiring and what I know will open the eyes of so many talents just fearing to make shit happen! I can't wait to read this all over again. Five stars!!!"

TAYLOR PRESLEY,
Co-Founder of Bespoke Homes

"*The Marketing Girl* is a bright and bold coming-of-age story that will have you asking why you ever did anything but exactly what YOU wanted, demonstrating what it means to quiet the noise and trust your gut—no holds barred. It's a funny, relatable, and motivational piece you'll surely gain something from . . . if not an entirely new perspective on changing the game."

KRISTA BRUGNONI,
Owner of The Celebration Statement

"*The Marketing Girl* is an excellent read that is not only relevant to the marketing and sales world but also contains valuable takeaways applicable to ANY discipline while taking you along for the ride on the ultimate journey of self-discovery. Any service-based industry professional, including those within the legal field and beyond, could learn important skills from reading this book and walk away a more driven, honest, intuitive, and motivated professional. Martina will have you laughing out loud while simultaneously lighting a fire under you to live your life to the fullest, proving that no dream is out of reach. Everyone needed this book yesterday. 10/10!!!"

MORGAN NAPIERSKI,
Associate Attorney at Woods Oviatt Gilman LLP

"Sassy, sarcastic, and the swift kick in the ass that anyone picking up the book needs to hear! Just one question . . . are you hiring?"

DEVAN SMALLEY,
Entrepreneur

"I loved reading *The Marketing Girl*! Martina is relatable and has an especially great way of making big goals feel attainable. Her raw storytelling is hilarious yet genuine. If she wrote a second book, I'd be first in line to read it!"

NA'EEMA MORROW,
Director of Marketing at Autopilot Recruiting

TABLE OF Contents

FOREWORD, xiii

INTRODUCTION, xvii

CHAPTER 1
BEAUTY SCHOOL DROPOUT, 1

Get Real, 3
Nepo Baby, 6
I Hate It Here, 10

CHAPTER 2
NOT A DUMBASS, 15

Favorite Angry Client, 20
Guitars on the Wall, 22
Business IS Personal, 25
Throwing Your Hands Up, 30

CHAPTER 3
NEW YORK CITY, 35

The Devil You Don't Know, 39
Better Than the Guys, 43
The "Assholes," 46

CHAPTER 4
MILLION DOLLAR BABY, 51

Play the Long Game, 56
Roller Coaster, 59
Dolly Parton, 61
Sparkly Success, 65

CHAPTER 5 — THE TEXT MESSAGE, 69
Golf and Cigars, 71
Not My Boss, 73
Looking for Sunshine, 77

CHAPTER 6 — THE WILD WEST, 83
Ducks in a Row, 89
A Fine Dining Restaurant, 91
Pajama Party, 96

CHAPTER 7 — THE W HOTEL, 101
High Risk, High Reward, 104
Eat Some Pizza, 107
Googly-Eyed, 111

CHAPTER 8 — PHOENIX, 117
Circus Acts, 119
Silver Bullet, 124
Nothing on the Side, 128

CHAPTER 9 — CEO, 131
Sexy, Smart, 134
Not Perfect, 139

AFTERWORD, 143
ACKNOWLEDGMENTS, 149
NOTES, 153
ABOUT THE AUTHOR, 155

Foreword

I hate being bored. Make me laugh, make me smile, make me mad, feed me, hate me, fight with me, *anything!* Just. Don't. Bore. Me.

    Martina and I have argued, laughed, cried, grown, and excelled together. I can say with certainty that if she is anything, she is *not* boring. The greatest superpower a human can have is fully knowing oneself. Knowing what you love, and knowing what you hate. Being confident in what you are good at, and not being too stubborn to delegate what you suck at. Laughing at yourself. Laughing with others. Giving your talents to someone and being kind to them without expecting an immediate return. Martina knows herself—and for that, we are all lucky to know her too . . . and lucky that she decided to write this book.

    I've experienced a little bit of success so far in life, but when I'm asked about it, I just say that I'm standing on top of a giant pile of shit garbage. I've failed, fallen, cried, questioned myself, had imposter syndrome, and then experienced a touch of winning. Rinse and repeat. And it's rare to find someone else in the world who shares these same qualities. Especially an Italian girl from Rochester, New York, when I'm a "hillbilly" from Southern West Virginia.

I have had the pleasure of knowing Marty for over half a decade now. What started as a business partnership ended up being one of my closest friendships. Which is how I think business should work. I speak a lot to other insurance and business professionals, and one of my main sales tips is to "just quit bein' weird." Meaning, just be your damn self. This is where Marty excels. Within two weeks of knowing each other, we were planning a giant event together in Dallas, Texas, claiming the other one was the best thing we'd ever met. Truth be told, we weren't even sure if the other wasn't a serial killer. (The verdict is still out for that. She probably drinks the milk out of the bowl after eating her cereal. Gross.)

I can guarantee that after reading this book for 10 pages, you'll see the effect Martina has. You can know her for five minutes, or you can know her for 15 years. Either way, you'll never be bored, you'll see what it means to be authentic, and you'll probably learn something about yourself as well.

It's my hope that as you read through these pages, you'll see there isn't a straight path. Hell, there isn't even a path. Life is more like a jungle that hasn't been discovered for 1,000 years, and you have to figure out a damn way through it. But it's worth it.

Read this book. Discover yourself like Marty has. Be better because of it. Let yourself pout—then, get over it. Go kick ass, but don't get too cocky. Chase a dream then change the dream altogether. It's okay not to know where you're going, but your ass better start walking. Reading my dear friend Martina Barley's story will help you get there.

Don't be weird,

TYLER BULLINGTON

Owner of KCX Consulting, Tyler Bullington Insurance in Huntington and Ceredo, West Virginia, and KCX Enterprises

Introduction

This is not going to be your typical business book. I'm not going to tell you how I wake up at 5 a.m. and spend two hours at the gym, sit in an ice bath, make a green juice, and arrive at my office by 8 a.m. I don't even like being awake before 8 a.m. There will be no advice like "Don't waste your time watching TV"—*Bravo* is one of my favorite hobbies, best enjoyed with a glass of wine. I won't tell you to keep emotions out of business. (People love to preach this as if it's riveting advice.) I actually believe that when handled properly, emotions can be of huge benefit to clients and staff alike. I have no structure or rules to share with you because I hate structure and rules. My only "non-negotiable" is having no non-negotiables.

Instead, I'm going to share the real lessons I've learned and the stories of how I learned them. I dropped out of beauty school at 17, filed papers in an insurance office at 19, waitressed at 22, and made six figures in advertising sales by 24. I managed salespeople twice my age, broke company-wide sales records, built marketing programs to serve thousands of very successful business owners (and some not so successful), hired and trained over 100 people, and presented proprietary digital solutions nationwide, all while running on iced coffee and a cocky attitude.

You know how most people who own businesses started with a well-researched and thought-out plan? They prepare for weeks and make sure all their ducks are in a row? My company, Uptown Marketing, started a little differently: it was an impulse reaction after my boss sent me a nasty text. To be clear, I'm not recommending that method. I'm just saying big moves don't have to happen perfectly; they just have to happen. Success can be about grabbing an opportunity, like when you get a text from your boss on a sunny morning that reads like a punch to the face. These are game-changing moments. You gotta take them and run with them, all the way to the bank.

And that's exactly what I did. There I was, 27 years old and really pissed off after reading that text. I'd just moved halfway across the country to Uptown Dallas. So, it wasn't exactly genius to quit my high-paying marketing career on a whim just to prove a point. But this point was important to prove. *I* would be the only one to decide what I do.

I flew into a CVS, bought a blue notebook and some of my favorite pens (Pentel R.S.V.P., give them a try), and went to the Starbucks below my apartment. The "business plan" I scribbled down was total chicken scratch. I filed my LLC, purchased a domain name, and set up a business bank account within two hours. People from my old company were blowing up my phone, trying to resolve the issue and convince me to change my mind. I mean, losing my sales talents would be an expensive hit. Almost three million dollars a year, to be exact.

Big moves don't have to happen perfectly; they just have to happen.

I'd been "the marketing girl" to my clients for so long—it was the only identity I knew. But there was no turning back for me. A lot of people would've had a little whiplash or buyer's remorse since, when the adrenaline wears off, it's natural to start questioning a big move. I was on track to make almost half a million dollars in commission that year, but instead, I ran headfirst into uncertainty with no clue what the hell would happen. I had no idea how to run a business, what I'd call my company, how I'd find a team, or how I'd get out of my tight non-compete contract.

Fast forward five years: my staff of 12 continues to grow, and my born-out-of-spite company is worth well into seven figures. I have nobody to answer to but my clients, just the way I like it. I've proved I'll always be "the marketing girl," no matter where I am.

Writing a book is like one *loooong* therapy session. A classic question that comes up in both is: what advice would you go back and give yourself? When I thought about this, I realized if I could somehow reach back in time and talk to 27-year-old Martina, I wouldn't tell her to do a thing differently. I honestly didn't learn shit in college; unless you're a doctor or lawyer, people learn the most from real-life experience, myself included. So, under no circumstances would I pull Past Martina aside and reassure her, "Don't worry. Everything's going to be okay one day." Nope, I'd grab my popcorn and watch her figure it out. Even knowing all the stupid mistakes I made, I still trust that little shit to find the right answers for herself.

You are the only one who decides what you do.

That being said, don't think I'm preaching to you or expecting you to make every move I made. No matter what stories I write here, you'll never be able to use my life as an exact formula for yours. Only *you* know the best decisions for *you*. Instead, I want this book to tap into that bolder, more confident version of yourself, whatever that looks like. Maybe you want to start a business. Maybe you want to buy a house or move to a new city. Maybe you want to ask your partner to marry you. You have to have some kind of idea (or dream, mission, ambition—whatever you want to call it) that lives in the back of your mind, but for some reason, you just don't go through with it. We see other people make these big moves all the time on social media, but we still hesitate to create the lives we want because we're scared of the unknown. After reading this book, I want you to feel *excited* by the unknown.

Rather than say you have to be crazily disciplined and set all of these unrealistic productivity standards for yourself, rest assured that you can have the life you want while being exactly who you already are. No drastic changes necessary. The only kicker? You have to *move forward* with what you want to do. Trust your intuition to lead the way. When you do, you'll find yourself confident enough to take the action that, deep down, you know you want to.

Don't freak out—none of this has to be done alone. I'm needy and clingy and could've never made it this far by myself. Throughout this book, I'll mention a lot of my clients because the relationships I've built with them over the past 10 years are invaluable. They're all smart, savvy business owners, and I'm even lucky enough to call some of them my mentors. I know I wouldn't be where I am today without asking for their opinions and guidance. Leaning on them, bouncing around ideas with them, and yes, even crying to them have been critical to my success. Amazing people like them exist out there for you too, so don't be scared to make those connections. I promise that you'll find people who *want* to support you and your development. Identify your own like-minded network. You'll be able to go so much farther with the right support.

I want this book to tap into that bolder, more confident version of yourself, whatever that looks like.

The quotes at the beginning of every chapter are my favorite pieces of advice I've gotten over the years. Turns out, insurance agents help the marketing girl as much as she helps them. I want to share all of that wisdom with you too.

Now, buckle up and get ready for some valuable lessons backed by the stories of a girl who went from a secretary to a sales superstar to a bold entrepreneur. I believe a lot of what we learn in business can also be applied to other parts of our lives, so I'll also throw in a little of my experience in real estate investing, some relationship talk, and a lil' general life advice.

All of the names in this book have been changed—because what fun would that be? The actual stories are the truth. Keep in mind: this is the *tame* version of it all. I legally can't write the tell-all that I *really* want—I'm not even kidding. By the way, if you're easily offended, put this book down now. I don't sugarcoat anything, and I can be very direct. You'll quickly learn how much I value authenticity, so I'm going to talk to you like I'd talk to my best friend.

Trust your intuition to lead the way.

The world is not like it used to be; our generation has broken the mold for good. Millennials, the first ones to grow up with the Internet, have taken over the reins, and now we're mixing stuff up. We're becoming the parents and the bosses and the politicians. And in this changing of the guard, we're throwing out rigid, cookie-cutter life plans, and we're *doing what we want*. Our parents may have felt like they had to go through life a certain way, but us? We're not scared to make a new path, and we don't really care what anyone else has to say about it. The only thing stopping us is the realization that *no one will do it for us*. We have to do it for ourselves.

After reading my story, I know you'll agree—if *I* can do it, you can too.

Chapter 1

BEAUTY SCHOOL DROPOUT

"I know good things are coming because I'm making them happen."

Let's start this when I was 17 years old, a junior in high school. I drove a red Dodge Dakota (thanks a lot, Dad), worked at Old Navy, and was absolutely struggling in cosmetology school. My high school had partnered with a cooperative education service to offer introductory courses in specific trades, cosmetology being one of them. My good friend, Rosie, was really passionate about doing hair, and I was really passionate about the idea of getting to skip four hours of school every day. We were in the same class, and all year, I watched her excel. She was the teacher's pet. Other girls looked to her for advice, and everyone knew she was meant for a career in beauty. Unfortunately, the same could not be said for me. I was great at the written tests, but anything where I had to actually *do hair* ended up a huge mess. I was a fish out of water when I held a pair of scissors or had to work on that ugly mannequin's head—I hated looking at that thing in the mirror. Before long, I started to dread going to class.

While it was cool showing up to school at noon and getting to "opt out" of my school's chemistry requirement, I knew I had to gracefully make an exit. My teacher must have known too because she very kindly asked me to reconsider coming back next year, saying that cosmetology probably "wasn't my gift." I loved musicals growing up, and *Grease* is one of my favorites. You can imagine my excitement when I literally became a beauty school dropout, but I was bummed that I had to go back to the drawing board. So annoying that I didn't have life figured out at 17.

The next fall, I walked into my first class of senior year, Business Ownership, and was excited to see one of my favorite people there: my junior prom date, Aaron. After sitting next to him and finding out that we had a hot new teacher, I had a great feeling about this class. I was right, but not because of all the eye candy in the room. I genuinely *loved* learning about all aspects of business, especially the marketing side. The more we learned, the more I loved it. We did a partner project where we had to make a complete business plan, and naturally, Aaron and I teamed up. We presented a one-of-a-kind gym-and-salon business called "Beauty & The Beast." You could be the beast while you worked out and then be the beauty while you got your hair or nails done. A one-stop-shop for self-care. Not to mention, it was an awesome brand name. To this day, I think it was genius. I don't know why I haven't opened it yet. This class was key for me—not only did I find a subject that really interested me, but it was one I was *great* at. For the rest of high school and into college, I followed my intuition right into marketing.

GET REAL

Listening to your gut will almost always steer you in the right direction. It's so normal to have moments where we want to fight our intuition: bad jobs, bad relationships, bad friendships. You have to pay attention to what you feel in every situation. Do you feel dread like I did when I saw my mannequin staring at me? Like a heavy chest full of anxiety, your heart racing in a bad way? Do less of that! Or do you feel energized and excited like I did in Business Ownership? Does it make you feel happy and buzzy and like you want to talk about it with everyone you know? DO MORE OF IT! I'm not going to sit here and say this is easy; in actuality, it takes a lot of thoughtfulness. You have to take time to get to know yourself, and that means pausing all the chaos of life to reflect. *You have to check in with yourself and be real about your feelings.* But it's worth doing, trust me.

Turns out, I wasn't interested in doing hair because I wasn't good at it. For some people, this would be a huge motivation to improve their skills and *become* good at it. But as a middle child, I'm competitive and I want to be the best—*immediately*. If I don't have a natural talent for something, it's impossible to find the motivation to do it. Which is why I don't vacuum.

I'd rather fill my time with things that I'm good at, even if that means figuring out another way to get my house clean when people come over. I've become so good at this in my life that Rosie used to tell me, "You do things differently than anyone else would do them. You always find a loophole or a workaround." Now, I've identified this to mean working smarter, not harder. Obviously, there will always be stuff that you don't want to do but have to do anyway. But for the most part, you can find ways to fill your days with tasks you're good at or *want* to be good at. You don't have to force yourself to work at objectives that you don't really care about or feel motivated by.

Too many people in this world don't enjoy what they do. Maybe they're really good at something so they feel compelled to keep going, or maybe they feel pressured by friends or family to pursue the same passionless goals. Maybe they don't have the confidence in themselves to forgo the easy route and say, "No, let me do this *my* way." If this sounds like you, you either don't truly know yourself, or you're ignoring your gut.

You have to check in with yourself and be real about your feelings.

If you've asked yourself, "What the hell am I doing with my life?" in the past month, stop and think about who you are and what you want (and I mean what you *really* want, not what you feel pressured to want). Maybe you've been thinking about a career change for a while. You don't have to start by quitting your job or cursing out your boss. Start with a simple list: write down the five main responsibilities you have in your role, and then sort those by what you enjoy most versus what you enjoy the least. Maybe you love analytical activities, but you hate talking to clients. The next step for you could be to look for a job that's less client-facing and more administrative, even if it's not necessarily your dream job. Changing your life doesn't have to be some huge, drastic decision. If you figure out what you like and then take action to fill your life with it, at least you'll be heading in the right direction.

If you see a task on your to-do list and think, "Yes! I get to do that today!" take note of that. If you do something every day, all while thinking of doing something else, then maybe it's time to consider that "something else." And if there's a part of your life you absolutely despise, here's an idea: don't invest all your time into it! Someone who hates space shouldn't shoot for the stars. Instead, shoot for what you instinctively *know* will make your life happier.

Work smarter, not harder.

NEPO BABY

Thanks to that Business Ownership class, my newfound love of all things business led me to make a change to my ever-growing career at Old Navy. I was now at the wise, old age of 19, and I wanted to be in a more serious business setting. My dad worked in management for a big insurance company, and one of his good friends owned an agency. My insurance experience was limited to going with my dad to Bring Your Daughter to Work Day back in the late 90s, but I was excited at the thought of working in an office. I called my dad from my freshman dorm room and asked if he could get me a summer job. His exact response? "No, but you can get yourself a job.

Here's his number." I called, and my dad's friend said I could start right away.

Don't be shy to use your connections to get your start. The whole "nepo baby" culture makes it seem shameful, but I am actually really proud to serve an industry that my father worked his whole life in. I'm also proud that I asked him to connect me with a great business owner who gave me a shot. That was my start to so much more. Identifying an opportunity through a family member or friend's connection is just smart networking.

I learned a lot more about my professional likes and dislikes at the insurance agency. I could very clearly see that certain aspects of business excited me more than others. Back in those prehistoric days of 2010, there were these things called filing cabinets. You used to put pieces of paper into different folders. (Paper is a thin, white sheet that has words or numbers on it. It was very popular years ago.) Papers piled up on everyone's desks, and I'd have to collect them and put them into the corresponding files. *Booooooring.* This office was also a little quiet, which I didn't really love. The walls were light gray to match the carpet, and there was rarely anything exciting happening. But I did really love everyone I worked with and the maturity I felt there.

Despite the grayness of business, one thing poured life into me every day: talking to customers. It didn't matter if they called in screaming because their auto insurance premium went up or if they had questions about a homeowner's claim—I loved it all. Connecting with people from all walks of life was so fulfilling to me. The opportunity to help someone when they were upset and make them happy again made me feel like a million bucks. Plus, my sweet, mama-bear coworkers always told me how impressed they were. I loved nothing more than hanging up the phone and hearing a "Good job, Marty!" Maybe I hadn't noticed it much then, but now it's crystal clear how important that kind of validation was to me—that's what pushed me to the top of my game. I wanted more praise! Not to mention, dressing up in office wear was also very fun for me. I felt so rich and cool wearing my pencil skirts and heels. Spoiler alert, I was *not* rich or cool.

I absolutely loved the women I worked with here; they were the best part of the office. I got so close to all of them. I would hear all about their kids and tell them all about my latest drama with Aaron. Remember him, my junior prom date from business class? He must've enjoyed that class as much as I did because, by the end of it, we were best friends, and he asked me to our senior prom. When summer hit, we were *seriously* in love. It got hard once we went our separate ways into college, but when we were home on breaks, we couldn't stay away from each other. We couldn't settle down together, but we couldn't fall out of love either. This went on for years. One of the women in my office always used to say, "You guys are meant to be, just wait."

I got to know my number-one strength at this office, and it clearly wasn't romantic relationships. It was people! When it came to people, I could go above and beyond expectations with ease. Not only was I great at solving problems and listening to our clients, but I genuinely enjoyed every interaction. Because I was so naturally talented, it motivated me to continue in client-facing roles. I followed my strength.

Someone who hates space shouldn't shoot for the stars.

I HATE IT HERE

When I was 23 and felt ready to leave my college job at the insurance agency, I went on a wild goose chase trying to find the perfect career. I probably applied to over 100 positions, most of which I was completely unqualified for. I tried convincing the director of sales at Entercom Rochester that I was good enough to skip past the entry-level sales position. He didn't agree. I tried convincing two sales managers at Lamar Advertising that I didn't actually *need* the "more than five years of ad sales experience" they required because I was *that good*. They didn't agree. My intuition was telling me that my marketing and people skills would be wasted in boring, entry-level jobs. And something in my head kept saying, "Keep looking. You'll find it!"

I turned down a job at a gym doing membership sales because I knew I hated the gym—there was no way I could convince others to love it. I turned down a job as the director of marketing for a collision shop because I knew it wouldn't excite me. I turned down an account manager position at a payroll company because, well . . . okay, I *did* take that payroll company job. But I only went for six weeks, and it was awful. Almost every college graduate in my city got recruited by this place. Operating like one huge corporate machine, they had a ton of different departments and roles, with me somehow ending up as a health insurance account manager. I felt like I was in prison every day I worked there. Again, everything was gray and quiet except, this time, the office didn't have five quiet people. It had 500. And these people did not talk to each other, like, *at all*. Plus, my "client-facing" role actually turned out to be super email-driven, so I couldn't even talk to people over the phone. I had no work friends and no motivation.

Every day, I walked into work thinking, "I hate it here." It felt soul-sucking and disorganized—the opposite of who I am. After six weeks, my anxiety finally hit a breaking point. One morning, after mentally working myself up to go in and make the best of the day, I got there and set my coffee on my desk. And then, I just kind of froze. After 30 seconds of staring into space, I picked up my coffee and left without ever saying another word to anyone there again. I knew better than to leave a job like that, but I don't regret what I did. It was just impossible for me to stay there a second longer.

Don't force yourself to stay in a situation that doesn't feel right. Instead, listen to the voice in your head telling you to get the hell out of there. My upbringing would have told me to "tough it out" and not just walk away; my dad especially always stressed the importance of "doing the right thing." Getting up and leaving sure felt like the right thing to me, and I'm glad I did it. Should I have sat down with my manager first? Yes, obviously. My dad is right; I should have done the right thing and left gracefully and respectfully. But I was young and dumb, so give me a break.

After I ghosted an entire Fortune 500 company, I was unemployed for 30 days. It was hell. I cried every day, feeling aimless and hopeless. I was too embarrassed to go crawling back to the restaurant I'd waitressed at. My life looked blank, and with no real direction, I had no idea what to do every day. I'd literally go take walks outside my house, just trying to fill the time. Not to mention, I was completely broke, I had rent to pay, and Christmas shopping was right around the corner. But *still*, something in me knew something good was around the corner. Knowing myself meant I knew I would be unhappy if I settled.

Paying attention to the dread and anxiety I felt in those opportunities told me it simply wasn't right. While I thankfully wasn't scared to trust my intuition, I could have just as well pointed the finger at myself. Seeing that I didn't succeed at the payroll company, I could've let that hurt my self-esteem. I could've so easily spiraled by thinking, "What's wrong with *me*? Why am *I* not good enough to excel in this role?" When you force yourself into a position where you're not skilled or passionate, you allow your environment to beat you down. Eventually, you start losing self-esteem and confidence, and before you know it, you stop believing in yourself. And where can you go from there?

The depressing reality is that most of us spend one-third of our lives at work.[1] So, if you're not picking a field that empowers you to be a confident, happy person, then you're screwing the other two-thirds of your life, including all of your personal relationships. People who do the things they know they're good at and like doing, though, will see the rewards of their work. Each positive interaction adds to our ability to make even bigger moves in the future. Maybe the people around us give out more praise and positive feedback, or we receive larger financial rewards. Every time we crush a presentation, win a big client, or whatever successes we're nailing, it all contributes to our self-image. Then, when we want to change our lives in an even more significant way—like buying a house or moving across the country—it becomes that much easier to take the leap. Every move you make will either deposit or withdraw confidence.

Don't force yourself to stay in a situation that doesn't feel right. Instead, listen to the voice in your head telling you to get the hell out of there.

Those 30 days of unemployment were a total nightmare of feeling lost and unsure, but I knew that after that one bad job, no way would I take just *any* position offered to me. No, I needed to be excited about the company, job, and environment. I wanted energy, and I wanted authenticity. Never again would I settle for a role I knew wasn't right for me. Someone somewhere would see my potential, and they'd let me show them what I could really do.

In early December of 2014, while my sisters and I decorated the Christmas tree, I applied for a position as a social media coordinator at a local digital marketing company, Bloom Industries.

Every move you make will either deposit or withdraw confidence.

Chapter 2

NOT A DUMBASS

"How can you become the best version of you?"

You know that scene in *The Wolf of Wall Street* where everyone's shouting and the phones don't stop ringing? That's as close as I can get to describing Bloom Industries. But before we talk about the salesroom, let's go back a few minutes.

I walked into Bloom Industries to interview for the social media coordinator position I had found on Craigslist. (*Craigslist*. That's how desperate I was.) At the time, managing the social media for a business seemed like a fun job, and plus, I'd already done it at the insurance agency. I was pretty confident I could do a great job, but I still remained cautious walking in. I couldn't accept an offer simply because there was one; I had to be intentional and look out for myself. I didn't want to work in another boring company. I wanted energy and excitement and that "good feeling."

Only five minutes into my interview, the tiny, Red-Bull-drinking hiring manager, Gina, stopped herself: "We can keep talking about the social media position if you want to, but I think I know a better fit for you. Do you want to explore that?"

Apparently, the sales manager, Nick, needed an assistant who could help him run the sales floor. I thought about it. It sounded important. It sounded exciting. And I wasn't going to blow past the opportunity of exploring a new option. I told her I would *love* to learn more. After all, what's the harm in that? Once I got enough information about this other position, I could easily turn it down if it wasn't a good fit. By saying I'd like to know more, I was showing my enthusiasm for the opportunity in a non-committal way. If there's ever a situation where you're confronted with a new experience that you're not sure about, let me save you from being indecisive and tell you what to do: *go check it out.* What do you have to lose? Maybe, like me, you'll discover something so much more exciting than what you bargained for.

When Gina introduced me to Nick and they showed me the sales floor, I couldn't believe Bloom was a real workplace. There were about 30 salespeople, some generating leads, the others closing sales, and all of them bursting with energy. A few were standing and pacing while taking calls; some were throwing a Nerf football back and forth. A short, blondish girl closed a sale, and she walked up to smack a huge gong, cueing loud applause. Two guys walked toward the back door, coffee in hand and cigarettes already in their mouths. The sales team was made up of the most bizarre combination of characters, from high school dropouts all the way to an ageless, mysterious old man who would soon share with me how he did time in federal prison for his role in a 70s telemarketing scam. I looked at the giant TV in the room that listed every sale for the day and the name of who made it. Everyone seemed genuinely happy to be there. This place seemed rowdy and refreshing, and that was all it took.

That's the thing about workplaces that instantly click with you. If just stepping into the building and seeing the staff makes you want to be one of them, you know you're in the right place. When you're trying to find the right culture fit, don't worry about whether or not they have pizza parties or casual Fridays; think about the feeling the place gives you. I instantly felt *excited* there, and I needed to be part of the madness. All I wanted was to work in a company that gave me validation, a space to grow, and made me feel excited to come in every day. Bloom—where people were being themselves, no holds barred, even if it was rough around the edges—fit everything I was looking for.

Nick wanted me to meet the CEO, Pete, before he officially hired me. I was led back to a huge corner office with guitars hanging up on the wall. Pete was a tall, intimidating Italian man, but he sat down across from me with a warm smile. The first thing he said wasn't what I was expecting.

"Do you have a boyfriend?"

"Yes," I replied.

"Does he expect dinner on the table at a certain time every night?"

I smiled, looking him directly in the eye. "I don't cook dinner."

I started three days later. Right away, I knew Nick was an awesome boss; he made me feel very empowered in my position from the first day. He told me that he wanted me to feel like I could make my own decisions, as long as I did what was in the best interest of the company. He also made it clear that if I did anything wrong, he would help me fix it. I cannot stress enough how this sent me running like a racehorse. I mean, I was a 23-year-old with little real marketing experience, yet he gave me all the freedom to experiment and do my own thing.

If there's ever a situation where you're confronted with a new experience that you're not sure about, *go check it out.*

Employers and managers, pay attention! The biggest way you can empower your employees is to do exactly this. Entrust them with responsibility. Encourage them to take initiative. Have their backs! Employees—know there are bosses like this out there. They may be hard to find, but they're worth going on the hunt for. They're life-changing.

Nick's immediate sureness in me shot my self-esteem through the roof. It erased all my fears of taking initiative because he made it clear he *wanted* me to make decisions on my own. He never micromanaged me and never questioned my judgment. Even on the days when I doubted myself, he reminded me of how good I was.

Nick built confidence in me from day one. He made me feel trusted, empowered, and valued. Then, he sat back and watched what I could do.

So, I gave Bloom Industries my *all*.

FAVORITE ANGRY CLIENT

I was crushing my new job. Nick saw I was a fast learner, fearless, and had a natural talent for interacting with people. Most of the tenured sales staff was hesitant to trust this young new girl. But Nick taught me the trick: no matter what, he and I had to support the salespeople. Just as Nick had my back, I had to have theirs. I made it clear that I would always be on their side. I knew I was "in" when they started coming into my office for help with their accounts. It took time and effort, but I earned their trust. Before long, my coworkers, who had been in the business for a lot longer than I had, started handing me the phone, and I became the go-to person for settling down angry clients.

Why did they come to me? Because angry customers sometimes need to hear a second voice, and I used my strengths of communication and empathy to truly understand them. I could easily convince someone ready to jump ship to stay with us, and a lot of times, I could even get them to upgrade. Even though I wasn't technically in a sales role, I was unintentionally honing my skills. I had already learned at the insurance company that persuasive communication was less about *saying* the right thing and more about *listening* to the client's needs. Over time, I became more adept at knowing which problems to offer solutions for and then showing clients the value in them. Even the angry ones. Digital marketing was new and confusing back then, and confusion can sometimes lead to frustration. I understood that most of the time someone was upset, it was because they were confused.

My first and favorite angry client was Pest Be Gone, a company in Charlottesville, Virginia. The owner, Mark, called in screaming, trying to track down his account manager who never picked up the phone.

"This guy sold me snake oil! I haven't heard from him in months! What am I paying y'all for?" I pulled up his account and started researching the notes while I chewed my gum and let him vent.

"Cancel my marketing immediately!" he yelled, and I realized that some damage control needed to happen if we wanted any chance of saving this. And it needed to happen *immediately*. Cancellations would go against the sales numbers I was working so hard to support. I started asking him questions and really, truly listening to his answers. Sure enough, he misunderstood what he'd signed up for. After an hour on the phone with me, he had upgraded his campaign and had my direct line. The account manager who originally sold him was blown away. Not only did I make his pissed-off customer happy, but upgrading the account meant *he* would actually make more commission from *my* effort. Talk about having the salespeople's back. I felt extremely happy that my efforts had mattered and that I impressed not only the client but Nick and the sales team. Pest Be Gone would go on to become one of the company's biggest accounts, thanks to my close relationship with Mark.

GUITARS ON THE WALL

Once Nick knew I was "not a dumbass" (his words), he made sure I attended meetings with the higher-ups: Helen, the director of operations who had *all* the say; Tony, the president; Joey, the CFO; and of course, Pete, the CEO. The guys were stereotypically big, Italian men. They reminded me of my uncles—big teddy bears, but when mad, they could roar like grizzlies. Everyone was scared of Pete, but he favored Nick, which meant he favored me too. Helen was the strict operational brain that usually had to reel the men in. She took notes, sat calmly, and braced herself for whatever was about to come out of these guys' mouths. Going into these meetings scared the shit out of me at first. I felt like a kid at the adult's table. But I wanted a seat, so I did the ol' "fake it till you make it." You know, pretending to know what you're doing while you actually figure it out.

For the most part, I would just sit there next to Nick at these meetings, taking it all in. I learned a lot. I saw the whole process of ideation, discussion, and narrowing down crazy, idealistic ideas into something that could actually work to grow the business. I saw some yelling and arguments, some laughter and hugging—there was no shortage of passion. This was where all the big decisions were being made, and I never knew what to expect out of a meeting in that huge corner office with the guitars on the wall.

The bigger part of my job was to help Nick actually *manage* people. And that did *not* come easy to me. In an environment like a sales floor where emotions are always running high and there are so many variables beyond anyone's control, managing meant being in a constant tug-of-war with the highs and lows. There is *so* much pressure and stress in sales, no matter what position you play on the team. Lots of emotions bubbled to the surface when things didn't go the way they were "supposed" to: frustration, anger, disappointment, and rejection, just to name a few. But the highs were unreal. We had set a goal to reach a "million-dollar month," and when we finally hit it, we popped champagne right on the sales floor and celebrated together all night. This environment seemed to bring out the best and the worst in people. Just not at the same time. I became addicted to this chaos.

$1MillionMonthPop Champagne

If Bloom was *The Wolf of Wall Street*, then Nick was, of course, Leonardo DiCaprio. He would run up and down the floor, yelling and encouraging people to dial like their lives depended on it. Me? I felt more like the girl in the movie who shaves her head for $10,000. But seriously, the yelling thing just didn't feel natural to me. Instead, I'd try to talk to them one-on-one and figure out why they weren't able to focus. This approach would work occasionally, but it wasn't nearly as effective as Nick's.

BUSINESS IS PERSONAL

As perfect as I thought this crazy job was for me, not everything at Bloom was sunshine and champagne showers. I had to deal with shit that I couldn't avoid no matter how badly I wanted to. Quickly, I learned how much I hated three of my major job functions: hiring, training, and firing. The whole process of finding employees, teaching them the job, and working with them to improve their performance was—I'm not being dramatic—*THE WORST*. I could not, for the life of me, understand why the junior reps found it so hard to just talk to people on the phone. To me, it felt like the easiest thing in the world. Just listen! Offer solutions that make sense! Make them laugh! It couldn't be any simpler.

One of the cringiest tasks I had to do was sit down and review recordings of their sales calls. No matter what feedback I gave, we saw little improvement. I'd estimate that two out of every 100 people have the talent to cold call successfully. Good luck teaching the rest. I lacked the patience (and probably maturity) to figure out how to motivate each person. Not to mention, the constant drama that comes with entry-level sales talent—late to work, disrespectful, unreliable—was equally frustrating. I found it impossible not to become emotionally invested in each employee, and every time they failed to perform, I took it personally.

Contrary to popular belief, business *is* personal. Ask Bethenny Frankel; she wrote a whole book on it. (Her book is called *Business is Personal: The Truth About What it Takes to Be Successful While Staying True to Yourself*. Give it a read. I highly recommend it.) Good or bad, I've learned Bethenny's right—you can't do it any other way. Don't ever let anyone make you feel like you shouldn't be a human with a heart in your career. It's all just a matter of when and how you let your emotions impact you in the workplace.

I've cried countless tears over employees who I expected better from. Whether they forced us into a situation where we had to let them go, stopped showing up, or just didn't live up to their potential, all of it crushed me. But at the end of the day, getting emotional over employees is not useful because, no matter how hard we try, we can't control someone else and their actions. That's why training was so hard for me—I kept trying to control people and make them do things *my* way instead of finding out how they could best do it *their* way.

Not being able to effectively train frustrated me way more than I'd like to admit. It made me bitchy, moody, or disappointed in myself, depending on the day. There were definitely many times Nick or Helen wanted me to keep my emotions in check. Having business conversations based on reactive emotions is simply not wise. I can't stress this enough: do not type an email while upset. You cannot think rationally while processing intense emotions.[2] Reacting emotionally to coworkers can also get you in a lot of trouble—I speak from experience. Since we were so close, I too often found myself yelling back and forth with Nick over a situation, desperate to make him see my point. Believe it or not, yelling in person is better than writing it in an email. At least you can talk it through and hug it out at the end, and you'll have no reminders in your inbox. As Dorinda Medley says, "Say it, forget it. Write it, regret it."[3] Of course, the *best* path is to communicate rationally and respectfully. Sometimes, that means taking a *looong* pause before communicating at all. It takes patience and maturity, which I was still working on as a 24-year-old.

I've had a lot of good therapists in my day, and the best ones will remind you that "two things can exist at the same time." Yes, emotions can be detrimental to your growth, but they can also be a key part of why you're successful.

During the same time that I was trying to control them, I also began to see my emotions as a strength. If nothing else, they showed me how much I cared about my job and responsibilities. Passion was what enabled me to kick ass and make such a substantial impact at Bloom. Without passion, there's just no way you can get a job done that actually turns heads and impresses. No one cared more than me, so I could use this emotional charge to go the extra mile to achieve for the sales team, for Nick, and for Bloom clients.

Chapter 2: NOT A DUMBASS | 27

Emotions are not *always* weaknesses; they're often an asset—they give you passion and empathy. Even the negative and poorly handled emotions teach you important lessons. Emotions drive you, and they can also steer you in the right direction. Don't try to ignore them; just get a handle on them. Channel them in positive ways.

Contrary to popular belief, business is personal.

All of this makes so much sense when I look back on it almost 10 years later. But back then, I couldn't even think about self-reflecting, much less do it. My only focus was putting my foot on the gas and making things happen. And when the people I was training were incapable of doing the same, I wanted to rip my hair out.

I'll never forget the first time I had to fire someone. Nick had been telling me for weeks I was going to have to step up and learn this "new skill." We often had to let people go; cold calling is not for the faint of heart. I'd always just sit next to Nick and stare at the ground while he fired people. He kept reminding me how I'd have to do it myself if I ever wanted to take over his position someday. (This was always something he dangled in front of me, in a good way.)

When Nick and some of the top sales reps went on a trip to Aruba, leaving me in charge, the perfect opportunity for me to take initiative landed right in my lap.

Rick was a poor-performing rep who was on our shortlist to let go, and he made the stupid move to come into my office and start arguing with me about yet another lead of his that didn't close. I was fried from running the sales floor by myself all week, and I kinda snapped. It was time to rip the Band-Aid off. Nick wanted me to take off my training wheels, and I just went for it.

"Rick, you're fired."

Delivering that fate to someone was not fun. I couldn't stop thinking about how he had to go home and tell his family he lost his job, all because of me. Unfortunately, it was just one of those things that I had to do. If it wasn't me who did it, it would've been Nick. It was in our job description. And while I'm all about not doing the things you don't like, there are unfortunately certain responsibilities you just can't work your way out of. I took initiative in the way I felt most comfortable with—winging it. Not overthinking or planning ahead and building up anxiety. Nick was *so* proud of me when he came back from his trip.

I don't think I would have been able to fire someone if Nick put me on the spot and forced me to do it. I had to come to the decision and take the action on my own. If a new responsibility is causing you anxiety, try approaching it from a different angle. Do it your own way. Taking control over stuff makes it way less scary. It was still uncomfortable, but as Nick always used to say,

"Get comfortable with being uncomfortable." That's the only way to keep moving ahead.

THROWING YOUR HANDS UP

By the time Nick left me in charge that week, I had built a good rapport with most of the sales team. Every day at work felt fun. They trusted me to help them, and I felt comfortable in most of my responsibilities. But there was still a major problem. Without Nick around, *they would not sell*.

The numbers were bad that week—like *really* low. Was it my fault, or were we just having a bad week? The owners would walk onto the sales floor at the end of the day, asking me what we had in the pipeline. Have you ever had four big, Italian men come to you looking for money? Not fun. I smiled and joked and tried to charm them into thinking that everything was fine and I could handle this. I was also trying to convince myself that I had it all under control. Deep down though, I knew this wasn't one of my strengths. I was competitive and I was bold, but I liked *doing* things, not waiting for other people to do things. I knew that in Nick's absence, this sales floor was my responsibility, so I had to just suck it up and do my best. I even had to run the weekly sales meeting by myself, which terrified me. I think it lasted five minutes.

The more the sales drought continued, the more I realized how severely I had underestimated the amount of motivation Nick brought. Sure, I was the cheerleading captain my freshman year, but I didn't have it in me to run around a sales floor jumping and yelling and clapping. That was Nick's strength, not mine. So, I tried it my way. I spent less time trying to spark group motivation and instead spent more time one-on-one with certain reps, pulling them into my office to talk. I went at it from all different angles—being tough, sweet-talking, playing to their big salesmen egos, anything to get them to pull some deals out. They assured me they would, but they let me down. I threw my hands up and counted the minutes until Nick got back to handle this shitshow. I officially wanted *nothing* to do with managing these people.

I know, I know—this story isn't inspiring yet. It's pathetic, but just keep reading.

Get comfortable with being uncomfortable.

One theory is that by working hard on your weaknesses, you can turn them into strengths. Eh, I don't buy it. Sure, it can happen sometimes, and if it's a task that's literally unavoidable (like firing people), then yes, work on it so you can *at least* be decent at it. But don't waste time on being mediocre at something you hate doing when you can be exceptional in something that you have a natural talent for. Management was my most mediocre skill.

You know what else felt mediocre for me around this time? My relationship. I'd been dating the same guy for a year or so. Sadly, no, it wasn't Aaron, whom I'd stupidly decided to end things with when we graduated college. It was someone else. Our relationship was fine for a while, but being in the real world hit us both differently. I felt less and less connected to him and eventually started caring a lot more about work than I did about him. He was on a different path and just couldn't figure out what he wanted. When he randomly told me one day that he was thinking about moving away, I threw my hands up and we agreed on goodbye.

Don't waste time on being mediocre at something you hate doing when you can be exceptional in something that you have a natural talent for.

Throwing your hands up is something you have to do to stay sane in life. We're told as kids to "never give up," but I don't agree. Give up sometimes! Some things are not worth the mental battle with yourself. Playing to your strengths means not wasting time trying to perfect your weak areas. Not only does this take energy away from what you're actually good at, but it screws you mentally. You'll be miserable and have *no* energy. Does Michael Jordan stress out because he's not good at knitting? Doubt it. Stick to where your skills are. Please take this with a grain of salt—I'm not saying completely give up on improving yourself; I'm just saying don't waste valuable gasoline driving somewhere you don't even want to go.

Ten months into my role at Bloom, during another painfully slow sales week, I threw my hands up again. Except this time, it changed everything.

Chapter 3

NEW YORK CITY

"Make a decision, and then make that the right decision."

One of the worst mistakes we can make is people-pleasing. I think it's just part of human nature. People fall into the habit of doing it so often that it affects every decision they make, whether they realize it or not. But think about it: you are the only person who can live your life. And your life is a direct result of the choices *you* make. Where you go to college will impact where you work, which will impact where you live, who you meet, who you marry, and who you build friendships with. If you aren't intentional about these choices, you could very well end up being one of those people who wakes up one day and doesn't recognize themselves: a middle-aged person unhappy with the life they've found themselves in. A mid-life crisis, if you will.

Reading this, you could be an 18-year-old who's ready to jump into life or a 45-year-old who's relating all too well. It's never too late to do what you want. We can change our mindsets at any age. Don't think because you've already driven in one direction for too long that it's too late to turn around. Al Pacino and Robert De Niro are both in their 80s and just had newborn babies. Do you think they give a shit what other people think of their choices?

Your choices should be authentic to who you are and the type of life you want to create for yourself. When you people-please, you please no one because you can't live up to it; it's not the real you. You'll eventually burn yourself out trying to make others happy. Do yourself a favor and focus on finding fulfillment instead of acceptance—others can either get on board or get out. I learned this one early.

It was the fall of 2015 when, once again, no one at Bloom Industries could sell. The two highest-producing sales reps were out: Paul was on vacation, and Charlie was having a major surgery. The sales board was scary low. Nick was in a mood, and the owners kept lingering around more and more, watching everyone with increasing scrutiny. Previously, when numbers were low, Nick would ask me to call the overdue renewals (existing accounts the sales reps were dragging their asses on renewing for another year). This time, I had an idea.

In an effort to boost our dying team spirit, I left my office and went out onto the sales floor. I sat down at an empty seat among the sales reps. I wanted them to witness firsthand that I was willing to work hard to increase our numbers and hopefully motivate them to do it too. I started calling the overdue renewals. Once I finished with that list, I told the lead-generating reps to transfer any business owner they got on the phone over to me. Yes, this annoyed the other closers because it was *their* job to take these leads. But they weren't getting the job done, so I didn't care. One sale turned into two sales, which turned into around $30,000 in sales for the day. To put this into perspective, an average sales rep at this time did around $50,000 for the *month*. Even *I* couldn't believe what I had done. I mean, it felt so easy and natural to be closing one sale after another. Was it beginner's luck, or was I actually that good? I did it all over again the next day, just to be sure. And *again* the day after that.

> ### It's never too late
> ### to do what you want.

By the third day, I was thoroughly enjoying myself. I could work a lot more independently, and I didn't have to wait around for other people to do something I knew I could do better. I felt *free*. I was hooked on the attention from my unbelievable sales numbers, and I was just getting started. Sure, my numbers impressed on the first day, but consistently fueling the entire sales board for three days in a row was nothing short of a miracle. Toward the end of the third day, the CFO, Joey, walked up behind me.

"Have you done the math, kid?"

"What math?" I asked, popping my gum and typing without even turning around to look at him.

"Have you figured out how much money you would've made in commission this week if you did this for real?"

I stopped typing.

I had not thought about it at all. As he walked away from me and into Nick's office, I did the math. The amount I calculated in my head was insane. And I had been doing it all without even stopping for a minute to consider it.

The money never motivated me, only the competition and excitement. I let them talk for a few minutes before I went into Nick's office.

On seeing me enter, Joey said, "You two talk this over," and left. It sounded like the two of them had already made some sort of agreement but wanted me to come to the decision on my own. Nick and I had a heart-to-heart. He was sad to lose me as his assistant sales manager. As much as I struggled, he considered me a valuable partner. Still, he knew that moving me into sales was the best decision for me and the best decision for the company. The only people who *wouldn't* be happy? The rest of the sales floor.

THE DEVIL YOU DON'T KNOW

This decision was a huge leap for me. My salary would be cut into a third, and I would rely almost fully on commission. Commission jobs are not always the most desirable; your income is completely reliant on you performing at your very best every single day. But I had unintentionally gone through a "practice round," and I knew that the combination of my natural talent and the adrenaline rush I got each time I made a sale meant that I would thrive. If you've ever thought of moving into sales but have that fear, ask if you can give it a try. Scratch that—if you've ever thought of moving into *any* role you're still unsure about, ask for a practice round. The worst anyone can say is no. And if they do, ask them why.

Of course, jumping into something new—mindset, job, relationship, routine—can be very scary. When faced with choosing either the devil you know or the devil you don't know, it's easy to take the familiar way out. But if you never choose to explore the unknown, you'll stay stuck in the same situation, which may not be where you're truly meant to shine. You probably know someone, or maybe you *are* someone who constantly complains about how they hate their job—trust me, you do not want to be that person who's too scared to trust their intuition and pivot into something new. Take your shot. Nobody knows you better than you do. When I took my leap into sales, I risked a lot, and as a 24-year-old with bills to pay, it felt terrifying. But I trusted myself to see it through. And I did. Nothing is stopping you from doing the same.

My first month in sales, I hit a number that only Charlie and Paul had ever achieved, and they'd been there for years. Charlie was incredibly supportive and encouraging because I'd always helped him out, and that's just the kind of guy he is. Paul didn't really care either way because he was so busy and focused. The rest of the closers, though, were beyond pissed. They complained about everything. I heard every version of "She's getting all the leads!" and "Why does she get the extra renewals?" Nick had my back though, being the great manager that he was. He continued to remind them in his not-so-gentle way: "Because she's closing them."

> **If you've ever thought of moving into any role you're still unsure about, ask for a practice round.**

Nick's philosophy was, "When someone is hot, keep feeding them opportunities." And I was on fire, so I became his go-to girl for numbers. I rarely had a day without at least two sales. My tickets were bigger than average, and my customers were always happy. Nick had every reason to keep me doing what I did best: earning business. (I guess it was kind of obnoxious; I mean, he openly called me his "shining star.")

In the beginning, the hate was not fun. The senior sales reps whose trust I'd just spent almost a year earning now hated me, either openly or behind my back. But most rappers would agree that your haters are your motivators. I wanted to continue to prove that I earned more opportunities because Nick knew I would make the most of them. I always showed my clients results. I identified their needs and offered realistic solutions instead of making promises I couldn't keep.

Sales dynamics have a lot in common with sports. Sure, everyone's on the same team, but each player has their own stats, contracts, and goals. And you still need to be competitive with your teammates if you want to stand out and be recognized as the MVP. There's only one star quarterback, right? In a sales team, it's even more complicated because your commissions are on the line. Only you are responsible for your success. The mediocre sales reps wanted everything to be fair and equal, but that's not how sales works. There is no participation trophy—it's "may the best man win." So, I made sure she did.

Take your shot. Nobody knows you better than you do.

If you are making the right decisions for yourself and your customers, don't ever let anyone bother you. I could've very easily given up or shied away from leads or sales to spare other people's feelings, but instead, I only got better. When my commission checks started rolling in on a regular basis, no one could stop me. Once they got used to it, everyone came around. Bloom really was like a big family, and they couldn't stay mad forever. We all had too much fun together.

BETTER THAN THE GUYS

Remember how frustrated I felt as assistant manager? Just the shift from being assistant manager to sales rep on the same floor made all the difference; sometimes, it's not about *where* you're working but *what* you're working as. I barely felt in control as an assistant manager, but as a sales rep, I could focus on myself and no one else. I didn't have to worry at all about the way others made sales. I could finally just direct all my attention toward making those sales myself. It was liberating and a total ego boost. I felt like a natural. This is where I belonged—no amount of coworker jealousy or hate would get me down. My numbers kept skyrocketing, all because I didn't care what anyone else thought. I only wanted to be the best.

But if I was gonna be the best, first I'd have to try to *beat* the best.

At first, my client roster was all across the board: roofers, attorneys, pest control companies, you name it. I even had a maple syrup farmer as a client. (She was sweet.) Charlie and Paul had been with the company for over five years. They did something no one else at the company did: they created their own marketing campaigns designed for insurance agents. While every other account got sent to the production department after a sale, Charlie and Paul managed these campaigns themselves. Insurance agents are some of the best salesmen around, which makes it difficult to earn their business. The only thing bigger than the billboards with their faces on them is their egos. Insurance was the big leagues at Bloom; Charlie and Paul earned higher commissions on these sales, and other reps weren't even allowed to talk to agents. But I never considered myself just another rep. And *hellooooo*, I had just spent *five* years working in an insurance agency! If anyone knew what made insurance agents tick, it was me.

Sometimes, it's not about *where* you're working but *what* you're working as.

Remember how I said Charlie was out having surgery when I jumped into sales? Well, when his surgery turned into a second surgery and someone had to step in to help, Nick knew exactly who to give his renewals to. I saw Charlie's insurance agents in my renewal queue one day, and I was ecstatic. This was my chance to be as good as the guys—no, even *better* than them. I immediately started emailing Charlie's agents to schedule appointments with them.

As the replies started coming in, my heart sank. I knew from my days of helping with customer service issues that Charlie didn't have the best track record with communication. But the responses to my emails were shocking. These people *hated* Charlie. He hadn't been consistent in managing their accounts and never saw his promises through. There was zero trust for me to work with. But I wasn't about to back down from the challenge.

One influential agent in Minnesota told me he felt duped, and after all but *begging* him over email, he finally got on the phone with me. I promised him I would work my ass off to turn his campaign around and make him happy. This was *not* an easy phone call, but eventually, he decided to give me a shot. I convinced a few more agents to give me the same shot while others wouldn't even stay on the phone with me for five minutes. Thomas Hebert, a prominent agent out of Texas whose business I really wanted to save, yelled at me for 20 minutes straight: "If they think they can send in the hot girl to bat her eyes and save the account, they picked the wrong guy!" I think I caught him on a bad day.

All this to say, don't let rejection stop you! I was mentally exhausted from getting yelled at by people I only wanted to help. Sometimes, you'll be held responsible for someone else's mistakes. This *sucks*. The difference between winners and losers, though, is that winners will step up, take ownership of difficult situations, and make lemonade. Be persistent, take challenges head-on, and do the right thing. This attitude will pay off.

I realized that customers were pissed off at Charlie because he never fulfilled all the promises he made. This made me extra conscious of what I told my clients. I had to set realistic expectations, and if a client came to me with outrageous demands, I needed to shut them down. No people-pleasing, as it turned out, also applied to my clients. People struggle to say no because they fear coming off as disrespectful or losing business, but nothing is more disrespectful than guaranteeing something and then not backing it up once the client has signed on. My clients began to respect me for my transparency. I was no bullshit, and they saw that what I said, I delivered. I didn't have to look far to see what would happen if I failed—Charlie's pissed-off clients were example enough.

Be persistent, take challenges head-on, and do the right thing.

THE "ASSHOLES"

After a few weeks of this beatdown, I realized that if I wanted success with insurance agents, I'd be better off getting my own and doing the right thing by them from the start. I wanted my own little mini-business, just like the two guys had. Charlie and Paul gave market exclusivity to their agents, so only one agent per market could work with them. They split up the markets, focusing heavily on big Southern states like Georgia and Texas. I sifted through Bloom's systems to see what markets were sold out. I remembered from my insurance days that New York City had some of the highest insurance premiums and, therefore, the most successful agents. I figured that would be the perfect market to find engaged, competitive agents who wanted to stand out. When I realized we didn't work with any agents from New York City, I went to Paul and asked why. He told me, "Don't bother with those guys; they're assholes. You'll never get anybody there."

I nodded, popped my gum, and walked back to my desk.

Don't tempt me with a good time. When the top sales guy tells you to steer clear from something, most people would stop right in their tracks. So, of course, I did the exact opposite. I just couldn't help myself. I printed out pages and pages of insurance agents in Manhattan, Queens, the Bronx, and Brooklyn. Instead of listening to his advice, I took it on as a challenge.

One of the profiles showed a younger guy with an Italian last name. I figured we'd relate, so I handed the paper to my best lead-generating rep and said, "Get this guy on the phone." Within minutes, he transferred him over to me.

Very quickly into my conversation with John Romano, I realized I was shooting the shit with one of the biggest agents in the NYC market. He had two offices, one in Queens and one in Brooklyn. This was a monster first agent to land on my own, but I felt no pressure. We got along great. He felt more like an old friend than a prospect. I learned he was older than his picture let on, but that didn't stop us from bonding like I had a feeling we would. Before he even officially signed up, he told me to call another agent, Camila, who needed help too. On John's referral, Camila signed up with me without hesitation. I was amazed and immediately felt a huge responsibility to them.

> 1 review
>
> ★★★★★ 2 years ago
>
> Martina has been fantastic to work with. She does not get threatened when I challenge her on information... but rather takes the time to educate me and support her statements with data. She seeks out added value to differentiate herself from others.
>
> She makes it easy to work with her. Oftentimes you find a rep who instructs you in all the changes YOU need to make in order for their service to be optimized... she did it all for me. She added further value by working with my team member to "school" him on how to modernize our Facebook page. She is informative, extremely insightful, and will break her back to make you a happy customer - even after the sale.
>
> I'm sure ▓▓▓'s great... but she is the reason I'm doing business with ▓▓▓. I highly recommend her services.

When you put your head down and prove yourself with hard work and results, no one can really stay mad at you for being successful. That's why I never ask for permission. Because then when I pull it off, which is almost always, I never have to ask for forgiveness either. While Paul was not in charge, he was still a company leader whom I probably should have listened to. But he was actually impressed at the risk I took—he knew exactly who John Romano was and what a big deal it was to get him as a client. Seek out advice from senior people, but don't take it to heart. If you feel strongly that you can be successful by taking another route, trust yourself and do it. I'm so glad I didn't take his advice. One way to forge a new path? Knock over the "do not enter" signs and keep moving forward.

I slowly signed on more agents of my own and kept chipping away at Charlie's old accounts. Instead of passing the account to Bloom's production department, I managed my insurance accounts personally. That's what both of the guys did, and it made sense. I trusted myself more than I trusted anyone else. I set myself up with a binder, organized each client by market, and kept track of what zip codes I gave them exclusivity in, who referred them, and other details about their business. John and Camila were both well-connected, each in different circles. They continued to give me more referrals, each of whom became an important client. I brought home my binder and worked on all my accounts at home, sometimes until

10 or 11 at night. My client list was growing, and it was growing fast.

> **When you put your head down and prove yourself with hard work and results, no one can really stay mad at you for being successful.**

I didn't give a shit about what anyone else thought and did it all on my own terms, my own schedule, and my own judgments. The reason Nick and Helen were okay with my slightly rebellious independence? I was outperforming most of the sales team. I had proven my bosses could trust me to do what was best for the company and my clients. Guess what? You can do this too. If you're exceeding the expectations of your job, you will be able to do it on your terms, your own schedule, and your own judgments. A boss who argues with *results* is a moron, and if yours does, you should start finding a new one. Especially if you're in a sales position. Salespeople need to be free to run, as long as they stay on course.

Now's a good spot to put the book down, take a stretch, and check your phone. We're at the calm before the storm.

> **If you're exceeding the expectations of your job, you will be able to do it on your terms, your own schedule, and your own judgments.**

Chapter 4

MILLION DOLLAR BABY

"People do business with people they like. Make sure they remember you."

You know that Ferris Bueller quote? "Life moves pretty fast. If you don't stop and look around once in a while, you could miss it."[4]

The next few years moved at such lightning speed that I couldn't have "stopped and looked around" if I tried. I went through another breakup, traveled to over 20 new cities, and my one-man-band of account management turned into leading a full team. My ability to adapt to change, think on my toes, and take quick, efficient action brought me to a new level. Never did I pause and think, "Wow, I've found what I'm supposed to do with my life." I just kinda landed where I was meant to land. So many people go through years and years of work without ever finding the right fit . . . and here I was. Being unapologetically confident in myself paid off. I'd found the perfect gateway to my career and jumped right in. As the days began running together, my adrenaline remained at an all-time high, and I went to bed every night thinking of what calls I'd make the next day. On some days, I'd have nothing on my calendar, and on others, I'd bring in tens of thousands of dollars. Believe me: you have to be a little sick in the head to love sales the way I do. You must be addicted to highs because there's no other way to make it through the lows.

It takes a certain kind of person to not only *make it* in sales but *enjoy* sales. The best salespeople are confident, client-oriented, and persistent. Charlie used to tell me, "Every 'no' gets you closer to your next 'yes.'" I loved that because it reframed rejection. For every client I failed to win, I felt like I'd moved even closer to my goal. Instead of letting the "no"s get me down, I looked at them like stepping stones to my next success.

A really important quality that was a huge help—more than even perseverance—was my ability to act without having to over-prepare (or really, prepare at all). Later in life, I'd take the ever-popular Myers-Briggs personality test, which has a part that measures how much information someone needs before they take action. More confident and aggressive personalities need less information, and more analytical and thoughtful personalities need more information.[5] These personality tests, as cringey as they sometimes feel, are really valuable tools to learn about yourself. If you've never taken any, start with the Enneagram test. I also love the 16 Personalities and the DISC tests. Dating someone new? Make them take one of these tests, trust me.

You have to be a little sick in the head to love sales.

Anyway, I learned from this test that I'm someone who needs little to no information before taking action. I thrive in chaos, and I love figuring it out as I go. Keep in mind: there are advantages and disadvantages to all personality types. My disadvantage might be your advantage and vice versa. Learn your advantages and lean into them! Flying by the seat of my pants always worked for me, and it worked well.

By the late summer of 2016, John Romano realized that a few other guys in his agent study group were also Bloom clients who worked with Paul. You're probably wondering, "What's an agent study group?" Basically, it's a group of insurance agents who meet up once or twice a year to help each other in their businesses. They'll plan meetings in cool cities and talk about their processes and strategies for recruiting, marketing, internal systems, and sales. Outside vendors are often invited to share their services with the group. John got Bloom an invitation to present at their annual fall meeting in none other than *Las Vegas*. This group was the cream of the crop—the best 20 or so agents in their entire company. Marketing was a hot topic, and we were driving results for John and the other guys. An invitation to this group was a huge deal. The stakes were extremely high . . . which was just *perfect* for Paul and me, who had never presented in person in our entire lives. He was hesitant to accept, but I wouldn't take no for an answer. Not even my paralyzing fear of public speaking would stand in the way of my ambition. Plus, I worried an opportunity like this might not come around again. We'd have the chance to network with many high-level potential clients, and I didn't want to miss this shot.

Every "no" gets you closer to your next "yes."

Tony, the president of Bloom, was an absolute pro at business development networking. He'd been establishing partnerships for the company for years. No one can work a room like Tony. He helped us get prepared, utilizing some of Bloom's best graphic designers to create an awesome presentation. Then, he sent us on our way.

That meeting was an important turning point for us. How many career-defining opportunities have you taken a risk on? How many have you turned away? Look back on the past five years in your career and think about these questions. How did they affect you? Are you forever a Lauren Conrad, the girl who didn't go to Paris? Taking chances may be terrifying. But the thought of *not* seizing opportunities should be even scarier.

By the grace of God, we nailed the presentation as if we were old pros. I must very clearly state: I was effing TERRIFIED to present. I wanted to jump back on a plane home. I almost threw up the morning before we went. Just to mess with me, Tony sent me a YouTube video of a woman completely bombing a big presentation. Though I was laughing, my stomach was in knots. But I had no choice, so I put on my dress and heels and went for it. Despite all my very dramatic, last-minute panic, Paul and I took turns, and I ended up speaking up a lot more than I had planned. It goes to show you: when you are confident in what you're talking about, public speaking really isn't that bad. (When I say it isn't that bad, I mean I *still* get nervous and panic before every single presentation, but I see it through.)

> Taking chances may be terrifying.
> But the thought of *not* seizing
> opportunities should be even scarier.

PLAY THE LONG GAME

As I'd hoped, this presentation opened up some pretty impressive doors for Bloom. One guy in the group, Campbell Enright, was a Vegas native and a bonafide celebrity within their insurance company. If he did something, thousands of his colleagues wanted to do it too. Luckily, he liked us, and he became Paul's client when we returned home. I landed four other very influential agents as clients, including the number-one agent in their company, Parker Brown.

Parker had a consulting business where agents would hire him to teach them his business practices. He soon enlisted me to help with the marketing and promotion of this class, and in exchange, he'd refer me to his clients in need of marketing services—a setup that solidified our strong relationship. I didn't ask anyone at Bloom for permission to do this; I just did it. If you identify an opportunity to help your client and your company at the same time, just do it. Sometimes, asking permission results in endless meetings before getting the go-ahead. Why waste the time?

Campbell sent both Paul and me *tons* of referrals. Although he was Paul's client, he also proved to be a great connection for me too. He was super supportive in encouraging agents from all over the country to work with both of us.

Networking is the lesson here! I didn't land this big opportunity or these big clients without being skilled at interpersonal connection. Asking questions, seeking advice, and offering value are key to making sustainable relationships in business. Meeting someone in person strengthens your bond like crazy. When you network in person, you don't have to launch into a pitch; just connect with them like a normal person. Ask about their life and share details about yours. Find common interests, and build a relationship for its own sake. Don't stand at a happy hour talking business unless the prospect brings it up. Just *make friends* with the person you're talking to. Doing business together becomes obvious once you have an emotional connection—people buy off emotion! So, if you're ever given the choice to do something virtually or in person, do it in person. There is no better way to connect with people than face-to-face. Bloom would not have grown the way it did had we not been able to network so successfully. Our accomplishments brought us confidence, and our confidence exuded when we met in person with clients and prospects. People are drawn to strength. (This is a Nick line—and a good one.)

Bloom always presented its top salespeople with awards at the annual Christmas party. I finished second to Paul, but I hit a milestone he'd never done: in my first full year in sales, I did over one million dollars in new business. I had actually hit the million-dollar mark in September, but who's counting? One of the sales guys started calling me the "Million Dollar Baby," which of course went straight to my growing head.

The next year was a whirlwind and ended with Bloom hosting its own agent event in Austin, Texas, in 2017. We had a two-day conference packed with outstanding agent speakers and some good, old-fashioned wining and dining. We earned lots of business that trip, including none other than Thomas Hebert, the guy who yelled at me two years prior because of Charlie. He was invited to our event by a friend, and he saw a lot of value in what Bloom had grown into. He even apologized for yelling at me! Once we developed a good relationship, he became not only my client but also a valued mentor.

I always tell my team: if you don't earn someone's business today, that's okay. It doesn't mean you won't *ever* earn their business. Don't be afraid to play the long game. Building strong connections is what's most important because, when people like you, they'll want to come back to you when the time is right. I've had a lot of clients come back to me years later. A piece of advice from a client I love? "People do business with people they like. Make sure they remember you." If someone chooses to do business with a competitor, that's okay! You lost; take it in stride. Try to identify why you lost, then improve on it. But either way, if you made an impression, they'll remember you when they start shopping again. Don't be the guy who's a dick when he gets turned down. Be the guy with enough confidence to wave goodbye with a smile and say, "Maybe I'll see you again soon."

ROLLER COASTER

Three days after returning from Austin, I must've been on some kind of high because I took a huge leap and ended another relationship. This time, I cut ties with a guy whom I'd been dating for about a year. We lived together and he also worked at Bloom, so you can imagine how tricky this breakup was. The following week at work, I can remember very clearly feeling so guilty for hurting him that I started crying while on a sales call. I told the prospect that I'd just broken up with my boyfriend and was having a rough day. I didn't care; I really couldn't hide it anyway. Being so vulnerable and honest, I broke down the wall of business formalities and built a human connection with the guy on the other line. This is the only time I've ever cried while closing a sale. Yes, *of course*, I closed it.

If you're in a client-facing role or any role that requires relationship-building skills, hear me out for a second. There is a fine line between being an overly formal robot on a call and spilling too much personal information. It's key to learn the skill of walking that line. It's impossible to build a real relationship by guarding yourself too much. Being unfiltered and authentic helps you build a strong connection so much faster. Do you have to cry to clients on the first call? No, that was extreme! But I've always been pretty open about my personal life to clients and coworkers alike. It builds trust.

Staying in the wrong relationship seemed like the easy option, but I knew that by finding the courage to get out, I could focus much more on my personal growth. Much like leaving that corporate job years prior, I knew that I should have ended the relationship in a more respectful way. But I couldn't beat myself up over something that was too late to change. Besides, I didn't want to change the outcome anyway. In my eyes, there was another bright side to my breakup: with no personal distractions in the way, I could throw even more energy into work. It no longer mattered to anyone how late I worked or how often I spent time after hours on the phone with clients or coworkers. I could do what I needed to do freely.

By this time, Paul and I had started to build a team underneath us. First, he got an assistant, the super smart and quick bartender, Hannah, whom Nick and I had hired into the lead-gen team a while back. Hannah was failing at cold calling, and I told Paul he should get her as his assistant before they fired her. I got an assistant next, then we got a shared support person, and eventually, we had a team of eight, all devoted to our insurance department. With the operational support at Bloom, we could leave most of the training to Helen and other managers. (By other managers, I mean my sister, Alexis, who had replaced me as Nick's right hand.) As an insurance team, we all sat together, so it was easy for our new additions to become immersed in what we were doing. They saw our high standards and hard work and followed suit. It was nothing like my prior experience in hiring and training.

> **There is a fine line between being an overly formal robot on a call and spilling too much personal information.**

We were on a roller coaster of traveling to study groups and conferences, coming back and crushing new business and renewals, growing our team, and continuing to build relationships. Campbell Enright kept us very busy. Every time he did a speaking event for insurance agents in a new city, we'd be bombarded with texts from agents asking if we had their market open. One month, we had business trips in Nevada, Texas, and California, all within days of each other. I was constantly being introduced to new agents: "This is Martina, the marketing girl. You should work with her."

DOLLY PARTON

With this growth, I pushed to take our internal marketing to a higher level. I wanted packages with catchy names and promotional materials with our pictures on them. Paul and I worked together to build additional products to offer clients. We both had different strengths and made a great team. I was back in that huge corner office with the guitars on the wall, except now *I* told them what we needed to do. As long as the sales kept coming in, they were happy to support us in any way we needed. They empowered us to make our own decisions—and they sort of had to, considering Paul and I built all this with no direction or leadership from anyone but each other. We were not trained by anyone; we created it ourselves.

Taking initiative and not waiting for direction is one of the most coveted traits of an employee. How often do you just do something instead of waiting to be told what to do? Go the extra mile. Look out for the best interests of your clients, team, and company, and then take action. Any boss who doesn't want that is nuts. Nick always used to say, "If you want something, take it." He didn't mean you should literally steal; he meant that if you have a goal, go do what you need to do to get it. No one's stopping you from working toward what you want. So, why don't more people have this mentality?

How often do you just do something instead of waiting to be told what to do?

I gave myself the new title of director of business development, meaning I would now take over the networking event planning and execution. I was already doing this, so I figured I might as well get a new title too.

I got us presentation time slots at study group meetings, industry events, and of course, our own conferences. I designed marketing materials and ran social media ads for Parker and his company, which brought us additional networking opportunities. I was great at building and growing strategic relationships. My best advice on doing this? Become a close friend who they can always count on to *handle shit*.

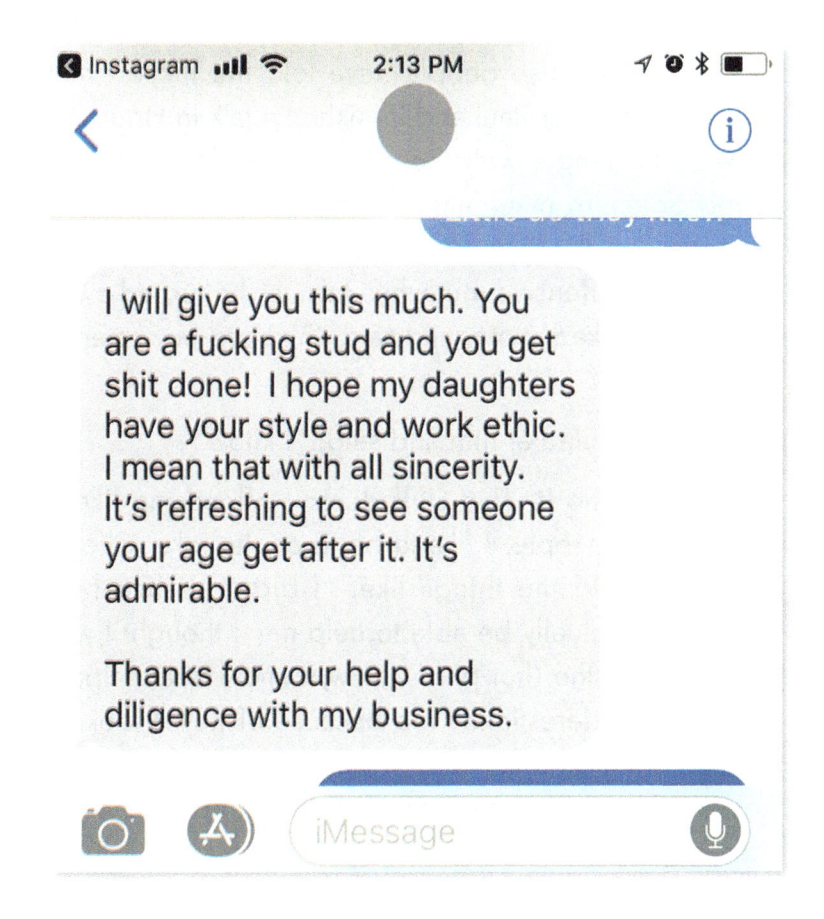

> I will give you this much. You are a fucking stud and you get shit done! I hope my daughters have your style and work ethic. I mean that with all sincerity. It's refreshing to see someone your age get after it. It's admirable.
>
> Thanks for your help and diligence with my business.

I always joked that I felt like a show pony at all these conferences. While connecting with so many people and presenting on a new stage in a new city, I sometimes felt that when Paul and I spoke together, everyone would look to him for the information but look to me as part of the show. Like I was the Vanna White of insurance marketing. By the end of the presentations though, those same people who first underestimated me would more often than not realize, "Hey, she actually knows her shit." I know this because people have told me these exact words. Once, after Paul and I finished a talk in Houston, we went to mingle with the agents over drinks, and a deeply Southern man came up to the both of us. Now, this man was the sweetest, and he didn't mean to be malicious or offensive. But while talking, he turned away from Paul, looked at me, and said, "You are way smarter than you look!"

I simply smiled at him and said, "I know."

I leaned into it. That stuff doesn't offend me like it does a lot of people; I like to be in on the joke. Clients have often told me things like, "I didn't realize how much you'd actually be able to help me. I thought I was just talking to the 'hot girl.'" Now, I know to anticipate that others underestimate me because of how I look or my age. Turns out, that's even better for me. The more they assume I'm inexperienced or incapable, the more I can absolutely blow them away. I did that throughout my entire time at Bloom, and I continue to do so now.

Women everywhere: stop getting offended so easily by people who are simple-minded. Poor judgment is on *them*, not on you. You are at a huge advantage by being a woman. You can complain about it, or you can use it. Dolly Parton very famously said, "I'm not offended by all the dumb blonde jokes because I know I'm not dumb . . . and I also know that I'm not blonde."[6] With this attitude, the joke's on them.

SPARKLY SUCCESS

When the insurance company that all our clients represented had a national convention in Vegas, five of us flew down for 10 days. You read that correctly: *we were in Las Vegas for 10 days straight*. It felt like another dimension, waking up every day in the fluffy Cosmopolitan robes and having room service on our balcony. Somehow, we thrived, hosting meetings by day and dinners or private tables by night. Parker took a few of us to race Ferraris and Lamborghinis at a track as a thank-you for our hard work. We went to champagne-filled parties with agents at Campbell's house. We nurtured existing relationships and created so many solid new ones. We came back with hangovers and *tons* of new business.

The next Bloom-hosted event was in Miami, just two months after the convention. I took the lead on the marketing and promotion of this event. I insisted we do a team photo shoot in a Miami-themed color scheme: aqua, hot pink, and white. The promotional materials looked *so* cool and made me proud to send them out. If you want to take ownership over part of your job, throw out ideas and then take action to make them happen. No one's going to argue with a really good idea.

I flew down to Miami months early to scope out venues, and we ended up picking an unbelievably gorgeous hotel in South Beach. If people were hopping on planes for this event, we wanted to make sure it was a place they were excited to travel to. Again, we lined up amazing speakers and invited agents from all over to join us for some learning and fun, but this time, we worked our whole team into our presentation so that everyone could see what we were building. We called the event "Work Hard, Play Hard," the purpose of which was to show appreciation for our clients and let them know we intended to keep working hard for them. We were pros by now, so we pulled off an awesome event and provided so much value to everyone who attended. This event is one of the biggest highlights of my career. To take an event from beginning to end is so rewarding, and there's nothing better than gathering people together to share experiences and have a good time. It was also my first experience in Miami, which is probably why it's now one of my favorite cities. It's special to me.

> **No one's going to argue with a really good idea.**

The speed at which we were moving only continued to accelerate. Our sales were through the roof—we were officially responsible for more than half the sales of the entire company between the two of us. My personal sales were almost three million dollars per year at this point. We were earning amazing commissions. Campbell had introduced us to some friends of his who were agents at another insurance company (which we'll call the Blue Company), giving us even more opportunities to continue growing our insurance department. I had even set up a meeting with a few of them in Miami, telling them all about Bloom and how we could help grow their agency.

I was seriously enjoying the ride we were on. I got to travel a ton and experience life in so many different cities, all expenses paid by Bloom. I had a front-row seat to endless conferences and meetings where majorly successful people shared valuable business advice. I could never put a price on the knowledge and wisdom I was able to soak in at such a young age. It felt like a way more elevated version of college—so much learning and so much fun. On one trip, I remember, in the middle of a laughing fit in an airport, one of us pointed out how we would someday look back on these days and miss them.

Everything looked like picture-perfect, sparkly success on the outside. Which made it really easy to cover up the cracks that were starting to form.

Chapter 5

THE TEXT MESSAGE

"Every interaction will either strengthen or deteriorate a relationship."

Had I taken Ferris Bueller's advice and looked around at the whirlwind I was in, I probably would have realized that my sanity and happiness were rapidly declining. Before we get into the next part, here's a disclaimer: I'm going to do my best to portray the struggles *I* faced and my thoughts at the time. I'll try to keep it objective. Do I think I deserved better from some of the people involved? Yes. But life doesn't always work that way. Sometimes, people disappoint you, and you have to manage your expectations of others. I know that I'm the one who has disappointed some people in their own stories. So, I'm not pointing any blame. I fully believe every person involved was doing the best they could in such a high-pressure situation.

When Nick was let go and Pete lost his battle with cancer, the entire company changed. Nick and Pete both brought such a motivating leadership style that you just *wanted* to impress them. I was crushed when Nick was let go, even though he was barely managing me anymore. The insurance team was separated from the rest of the sales team by now, but he was always a safe space for me there. No one had my back the way he did. So, once he was gone, I couldn't help but feel like I was on my own.

GOLF AND CIGARS

Tony was the last man standing at the leadership level of the sales and insurance teams. Paul and I were pretty self-led, so it was less about day-to-day management and more about providing us with the tools we needed to keep being successful. He helped support us in our events and taught us skills in entertaining clients. I loved Tony like an uncle, but for whatever reason, I felt he never took me seriously. And this feeling only grew. While I was a part of all the bigger department meetings, I noticed, after Miami, that Tony began taking more one-on-one meetings with Paul alone. They'd golf and smoke cigars together, and to say I had FOMO would be an understatement. I knew how these games worked, and I got the sense that something major was happening, something that I wouldn't like one bit. And I was right.

Paul and I worked really well as partners . . . until we didn't. Which was around when Paul was promoted to the head of the insurance department. Sure, he had worked at Bloom for many years and had a long list of clients. But the insurance department would have never come close to what it grew into without me stepping in and taking it to the next level. I had busted open brand new markets, added a huge number of insurance agents to the Bloom roster, took initiatives to get us networking opportunities, and developed processes that helped us grow so much. Our sales were neck and neck by this point. I really saw us as partners in our success, so I was deeply hurt when he was promoted and I was left behind. Despite Paul and I being equals, I noticed a shift in my relationship with Tony. I was still valued as a great salesperson, but I was not looked at as someone to be pulled up to the next level. I felt like a little sister trying to prove she could keep up with her big brothers.

I was being pushed out of the loop. Decisions and moves were made without my input, and changes concerning me took place without me being notified. Suddenly, there were two totally inexperienced new sales reps who were supposed to sell to the Blue Company. Even though I had made the connections and taken the meetings, I wasn't allowed to take any of the Blue agents on as clients. I had to call the agents I met with in Miami to tell them I couldn't handle their accounts and introduce them to the brand-new guy who would take them. It was gut-wrenching not to be able to handle the accounts I had secured, and I hated the thought of people with no experience being responsible for the agents' success. But what felt even worse was not to be acknowledged or appreciated for everything I had done.

Paul was now "in charge" of every employee in the insurance department. I'd given myself that new title, but I had just made that up—it wasn't a real promotion and definitely didn't come with any increase in pay or authority. I frequently expressed to Tony and Helen that I felt I deserved a promotion too. Tony would laugh and say, "I just need you to shut up and sell." I distinctly remember another line he used: "You're like my ATM. I could stick my card in your mouth and money would come out!" I laughed it off, knowing Tony had a big mouth, but he didn't have malicious intent. Still, it confirmed where my place was. I'd spent years dedicated to opening up and maximizing new opportunities so Bloom could explode in growth—but despite all the hard work and initiative I put in, I got no recognition for this. As Tony so eloquently put it, I was nothing more than an "ATM" for Bloom. Yet Paul, who did the exact same job as me, was promoted. Resentment and bitterness started to accompany me to work every day. I challenged any decision made by Paul, Tony, or Helen. My attitude toward them was terrible. I never stopped putting in the effort, but I did start noticing how much it was taken for granted.

NOT MY BOSS

These negative feelings carried over to my life outside Bloom too. And since my social life and Bloom overlapped, as it often did at parties and events, it reached a boiling point. Once, at a mutual friend's birthday dinner, Paul and I got into yet another argument. Paul, who could never pass up an opportunity to take a stab at me, drunkenly announced in front of 10 of our friends that he was getting paid extra commission off of *my* sales. I immediately saw red and started yelling. Our screaming match reached an absurd level, and we ruined the dinner for everyone. One of us accidentally knocked over a glass of red wine,

Chapter 5: THE TEXT MESSAGE | 73

and by that point, no one was in the mood for birthday cake. I felt guilty for wrecking everyone's night, but I felt so out of control. I couldn't figure out how to gain the acknowledgment and respect that I felt I deserved.

Why was *he* getting paid for *my* sales? Sure, usually sales managers take a cut of the sales made by the salespeople under them. That's how the structure worked for Nick who, as the sales manager, earned a percentage from any sale made by a closer on his floor. But that was a different matter for one big, all-important reason—*Nick trained them*. He put in the hard work to motivate the salespeople and worked with them until they shined. The same could not be said for Paul, especially when the salesperson was *me*. He had no input in what I did, he didn't contribute in any way to my sales, and I didn't take direction from him. And thank God I didn't—remember when he told me to stay away from New York City agents? We had completely different styles anyway. I was happy to keep at it on my own—I didn't need training. I was mad enough that he was promoted over me, but finding out that he was making money off of my sales was just one more slap in the face. My ego could not take it, so I refused to acknowledge his promotion or look at him as any type of leader. I made it clear to everyone: "Paul is *not* my boss. He is *not* responsible for my success in any way, shape, or form."

I can't blame Paul for taking the promotion. If it'd been offered to me instead of him, I sure as hell wouldn't have said, "Wait, what about Paul?" In his mind, he'd put in way more years than me, working with insurance agents. In my mind, I'd driven *more* results in less years. Have you ever been passed up for a promotion or anything similar? It sucks. I don't even have good advice for you because I didn't take it gracefully. I acted like a little brat. Looking back, what could I have done differently? I honestly don't know. I could say that I should have just put my head down, continued being a leader, and kept a good attitude. But I really wasn't in the right environment. Something about the way Tony and Paul acted toward me felt really condescending, which was ironic because there were so many situations where it was *my* actions that led our team to success.

At the same time that work became more and more maddening, my personal life continued to become more depressing. I was still single, bored as hell most of the time, and very lonely. My social life was so intertwined with Bloom that when I went to a bar or party, it was most often with people from work. There seemed to be no boundaries, and I was constantly in a state of mind where I could think of nothing but Bloom. After all, when I saw the same people and had the same conversations no matter where I turned, it was hard to find anything else to think about. My dating life was pretty inconsistent for the same reason. I would go out on a date once in a while, but then I just couldn't deal with it. Some guys were left permanently waiting for a text back from me. I had no energy to give—for a partner or for myself. The only person I hung out with outside of Bloom was my trainer, who I basically paid to be my friend. I mean, I *hate* working out. I even got a puppy, thinking it would cure my loneliness. Within a week, the rambunctious, slobbery dog found a new home at my little sister's.

If you had asked me then what my work-life balance was like, I would've just laughed and asked you what that meant. I'm not one of those people who can clock out at five and go home. That's just not who I am. Which brings me to something I want to stress: there's no perfect work-life balance routine. Something that works for you won't necessarily work for someone else. And as you get older, your idea of work-life balance will likely shift. Back then, I wasn't in a relationship, and I didn't have any kids, pets, or real responsibilities in life. I knew many people who were in serious relationships and starting to have babies, and they treated their personal time with much more value. Not everyone's idea of a good work-life balance will look the same.

Assess what *you* want out of this time in your life. Are you in ass-kicking mode? That's awesome; spend more time at the office! Put that work in now. Do you value time with your spouse and kids? Go enjoy your family! That's what you're working for, after all. All I wanted then was to make my clients happy and make sales, so working my butt off day and night didn't feel like I was missing out on anything. In my own way, I had achieved a balance.

> **There's no perfect work-life balance routine. Something that works for you won't necessarily work for someone else.**

These are all, of course, my reflections in hindsight. At the time, I did what I wanted—even though I didn't think much about *why* I wanted it—and channeled my mental energy toward work. Despite how chaotic, thankless, and frustrating my job might have seemed, I loved the work itself. I had a very real passion for helping my clients and succeeding in my goals. Although I fell into a constant state of overstimulation, I embraced it and used it as a springboard to keep pushing forward and outpace everyone around me. But with Paul's promotion and our power struggle that I was definitely losing, I was on the brink of insanity—more so than usual. I knew if I didn't shift gears somehow, I'd end up in a really bad place. When you feel you want a change, it's usually because you *need* one. So, don't ignore it.

LOOKING FOR SUNSHINE

It was January 2019, and we were in the middle of a snowstorm.

My assistant-turned-close-friend, Ava, texted me a picture of some football player's girlfriend on Instagram who lived in Houston. When you're sitting in bed on a gloomy winter day, a picture like this can really make you think. It starts to feel like even the littlest bit of sunshine could solve all your problems.

She texted, "Could you imagine if we lived this life?" The same thought was going through my head. What would it be like to live somewhere so warm and sunny and beautiful? No one said we couldn't just pack our bags and move. All that was in the way was . . . well, nothing.

"Let's go find an apartment," I replied.

When you feel you want a change, it's usually because you *need* one.

I was at a low point at the time—mentally and professionally—so I realized I needed some space. Literally. I decided to physically remove myself and move miles and miles away and get all the space I needed. The next weekend, we were in Texas and shopping for apartments. Big moves require action, not just talk. We could've gone back and forth forever wishin' and hopin' and thinkin' and prayin', but like the song says, that won't get you into his heart. Or into a new life. We booked a flight, set up appointments to look at apartments, and decided to sign a lease before leaving. I listed my house for sale and even held an "estate sale" where my friends dressed up in "estate staff" outfits to help me downsize and sell a lot of what I didn't need. I found someone from my gym who was willing to drive a U-Haul full of my stuff all the way down to Texas for way cheaper than movers would have.

Thirty days later, I was all moved into the big, beautiful apartment in Uptown Dallas that Ava and I shared. I felt like I could finally breathe. Even though I had lived in my own house in Rochester, it was too massive for one person and only made me feel that much lonelier. It was a house but never a home. The only reason I'd built it

Chapter 5: THE TEXT MESSAGE | 79

was because I was sick of listening to my dad tell me how I should be investing my money. I felt withdrawn and bored by myself at home, which is why I preferred to stay late at work instead. Everyone told me I was crazy when I went to sell the house only a year or so after having it built. Even in that short time, I made a *goooood* chunk of money selling it. This was my first taste of the opportunity in real estate.

Sharing an apartment with a girlfriend was a welcome change. Every day in Texas was bright, the people were so friendly, and there was so much to do. The unknown felt exciting and full of hope—and before I knew it, my mental health began to recuperate and feel replenished by the change.

Of course, packing up and moving away may not be an option for everyone. I was in a position in my life where I had the financial means to do it and nothing tying me to stay in Rochester. If you feel like you need a change, you don't need to do something this drastic and crazy. Everybody has a different tolerance to change— knowing yours can help you make decisions that provide comfort rather than anxiety. No matter how big or small of a change you end up making, the important part is to just *do it*. Don't stay in a bad job, bad relationship, or a bad situation just because it's scary to venture into something new. Sometimes, even a seemingly inconsequential change can make a huge difference. Other times, you'll have a moment when all you can do is throw your hands up, admit that something isn't working, and take the plunge with a choice you know will improve your life. So, when an unexpected door opens—like my chance to move to Dallas—take it. What's the worst that could happen? I figured, worst case scenario, I'd move back.

Big moves require action, not just talk.

When I moved, Tony and Helen were more than happy to let me work remotely since they were probably sick of dealing with all the bullshit between Paul and me anyway. I personally paid for my own office space in a high-rise on McKinney Avenue. Bloom mailed me a computer, monitor, and mouse. I set up my little workspace, and everything was going great. For exactly seven business days.

Wednesday, March 12, 2019, started out the same as any day in my new Dallas life. I woke up, got ready, walked down to Starbucks, and ordered a venti cold brew with almond milk. I walked to my office, sat my big coffee down, and started firing off emails. My phone lit up—a text from an agent who said he got my number from one of my clients, apparently a friend of his. He'd heard about Bloom and wanted my help. After a 20-minute phone call, he signed up with me. I finished his onboarding and called my assistant back home to give her the details of our new client. Then, I wrapped up some other little tasks and headed back to my apartment.

I remember every detail of this day, except I can't remember why I was in the car. I only know that I was driving when my phone started blowing up with rage texts from Paul. He thought that my newest client should have been *his* account since the guy was somehow connected to one of Paul's clients. I told him something along the lines of, "Tough shit. He's friends with my client too. He didn't reach out to you." I sent him screenshots of the guy texting *me* directly and asking to work with *me* specifically. We went back and forth, each message nastier and more aggressive than the next.

I was still in my car when Helen texted me to stop communicating with Paul, saying that we would "figure it all out."

Yeah, I thought, *like I can trust that.*

I told her that there was nothing to figure out, that Paul needed to leave me alone, and that I would continue helping agents who reached out to me. My phone lit up again with another message from Helen:

"You work for Bloom Industries, and Tony and I will decide what you do or do not do."

> You work for Bloom Industries, and Tony and I will decide what you do or do not do.

Chapter 6

THE WILD WEST

"You're never gonna lose when you bet on yourself."

For the next few hours after receiving that text, I ran on pure adrenaline and more cold brew. Something about reading those words made me instantly realize my time at Bloom was over. I could do this on my own.

My blue notebook was soon filled with scribbled notes on my new business: who I would hire, what I would offer, and how I would put it all into action. The name took some thought, but as a new resident of Uptown Dallas, I decided on Uptown Marketing. I filed an LLC, set up a business bank account, and got my tax ID. I changed all of my passwords that gave Bloom access to my client accounts. Helen had the audacity to send me another text once I put them in this bind, saying she wasn't sure how it had escalated to this level. That still makes me laugh almost five years later.

It was time to start talking to my two ideal teammates.

Samara had been one of my best friends since our early 20s. We bonded over the fact that my fourth-grade boyfriend ended up being her high-school boyfriend. We always said he had great taste in girlfriends. A few years prior, I hired Samara at Bloom, and she was just as miserable there as I was toward the end. She kept begging me to start my own company, saying she'd be the first to join. When I resigned, she put her notice in almost immediately. Her unwavering confidence in me gave me a lot of strength. I had to make this successful. Not just for me and my future, but for Samara and her future as well.

Mona, my cousin who is more like a sister, was the obvious next choice. Her analytical brain was everything I lacked but everything I needed if I wanted any chance of success. Her attention to detail is unmatched, and our close bond had worked for us in a professional setting twice before. She's the right brain to my left brain; together, we could make anything happen. While I already knew we made a great team, Mona needed some convincing—she wanted all the details and a formal offer letter. Once she saw I was dead serious, she jumped in with Samara and me.

We went full speed ahead, but one massive obstacle still stood in the way. When I started at Bloom as a young, wide-eyed 23-year-old, I had signed a non-compete agreement. At the time, I had no idea what I was signing nor did I really care. But now, it was coming back to bite me in the ass. The overly strict contract stated that upon leaving Bloom, I couldn't work in any form of marketing, anywhere in the country, for at least two years.

When I found out, I realized what a crushing amount of responsibility lay on my shoulders. Both Mona and Samara, two of my closest friends, had left their jobs to work with me. And if I couldn't find a workaround to launch my new business, they would have no way to support themselves. Plus, I had just signed a lease on a new apartment using my old Bloom income, which I obviously wasn't receiving anymore. So, there was a lot riding on Uptown even before it officially started. But with so much at stake, sometimes all you can do is let confidence take the wheel. Mona and Samara had the confidence that I'd be able to make a success out of Uptown, and I had confidence in myself. There was no plan B if Uptown didn't work out. But who needs a plan B when it's an all-or-nothing situation? After all, I thrive in chaos. Without that kind of pressure, it wouldn't be as exciting when I pulled it off, would it?

Unphased by the drama I'd found myself in, my roommate, Ava, was quick to step up and help. She used to bartend at a ritzy place back in her college days in Tampa, and one of her regulars was a high-profile attorney. She frantically started texting, and within the hour, I was connected with a very expensive, very aggressive attorney out of New York City: Maxwell Peterson.

Maxwell was *way* overqualified for the job but more than happy to accept my large retainer payment, which I paid for with the cash I earned from selling my big, lonely house in Rochester. He told me to look at the retainer as a business investment—because if I didn't get out of the non-compete, I wouldn't have a business at all. He talked incredibly fast in a thick New Yorker accent, and any time I'd call him begging for updates, he'd give a couple of quick words and interrupt my worries with, "We're good. We got it. We got this." I'm certain my little negotiations were nothing in comparison to his other high-profile clients. I mean, he was a CNN analyst. But Maxwell still took the time to assure me that Bloom didn't stand a chance against him. When Bloom didn't pay me a check I was owed, he moved at lightning speed to get them to pay me. Anytime he was up to the plate, he knocked it out of the park. I reached out to him in March, and by August, we signed, sealed, and presented Bloom with a proposal that would work for both parties: I would not pursue Bloom clients for two years, but if anyone came to me on their own, I could take them.

Thank God for social media. Once I posted about my new company, my old clients immediately started texting and calling. Business was coming in.

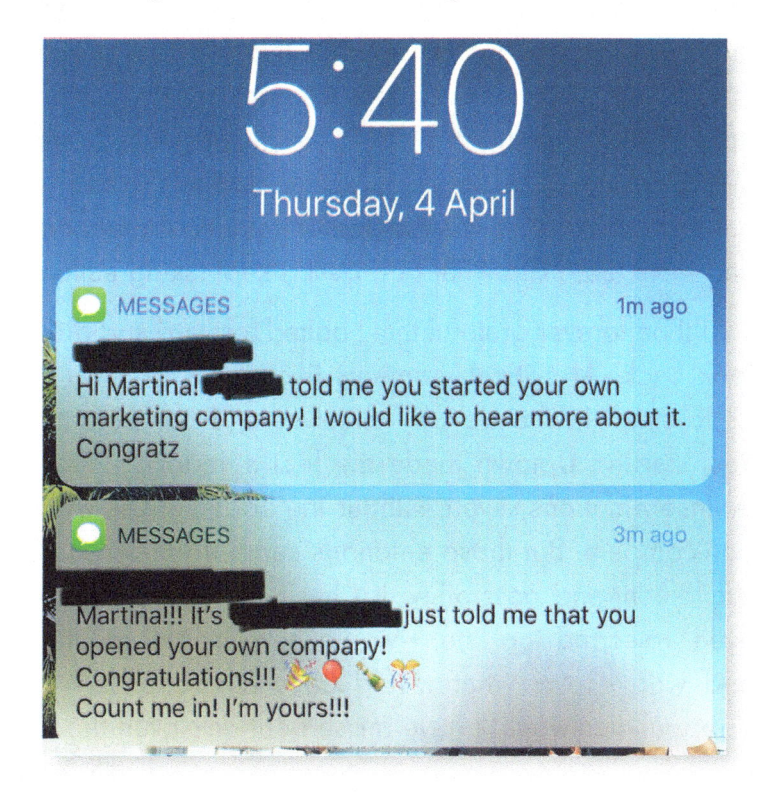

> **5:40**
> Thursday, 4 April
>
> MESSAGES — 1m ago
> Hi Martina! ▇ told me you started your own marketing company! I would like to hear more about it. Congratz
>
> MESSAGES — 3m ago
> Martina!!! It's ▇ just told me that you opened your own company! Congratulations!!! 🎉🎈🍾🎊
> Count me in! I'm yours!!!

But in that long five months of legal negotiations, I didn't just sit back and wait for the go-ahead. From the day I quit Bloom, I moved forward as if the non-compete agreement didn't exist. I had to keep going, and nothing would stop me. After what I'd paid Maxwell, I figured the agreement was his problem to deal with. Of course, people kept warning me to slow down, but I physically cannot go at anything other than "full speed." I didn't have time to sit around and wait for attorneys to go back and forth for months; I had a business to get off the ground. Instead, I had to take a huge—but calculated—risk. These are the times when you have to ask, "What's the worst that could happen?" In this situation, I knew that the worst-case scenario was the non-compete holding up and Bloom suing me. Pretty rough worst-case, but I liked my odds. Maxwell assured me that this would not happen, backing up his statements with legal precedent and facts. So, I did what I do best: I kept taking action.

I'll be forever grateful that I bolted forward and didn't look back. At critical moments like these, it's easy for us to stand in the way of ourselves and our potential. Yes, starting Uptown made me feel a variety of scary, intense emotions, even without the added stress of the non-compete. But those emotions came from a place of excitement and possibility. If I hesitated and waited for even a second too late, I would have lost momentum, and who knows what would have happened? What opportunities would I have missed out on? Even though

I charged straight in, I was still careful not to approach Bloom clients, allowing them to approach me instead. Thankfully though, because of the close relationships I had with so many, it didn't take long for them to reach out to me.

Can I just say how non-competes are the worst? Unless you're dealing with C-suite employees and super top-secret company information, what the hell are they for? No one can work for any company but yours? Companies should worry more about retaining employees instead of finding ways to restrict them if they leave. It's like a bad prenup.

DUCKS IN A ROW

John Romano was the first Uptown Marketing client. Because we talked so often, he reached out one day, and I didn't waste any time telling him that I'd left Bloom. He didn't question my decision for a second nor did he ask about Uptown's plans, offerings, or prices. Instead, he just asked, "What do you need for me to switch to Uptown?" Always my most loyal client, John proved what I had been so sure of—most of my clients wanted *me*; they didn't care what company I worked for. John had become like a big brother to me at this point. He had been in business for a long time and was (still is) always just a phone call away when I needed anything.

The next client who got on Uptown's roster was Thomas Hebert. Thomas had become a mentor to me over the years, and he was absolutely paramount in helping me learn to channel my emotions into positive action. Whenever I struggled at Bloom, he would usually talk me through the problem and teach me the most effective way to handle it. I didn't feel I had anyone to turn to for leadership at that company after Nick left, but that didn't stop me from finding guidance in clients like John and Thomas. If I hadn't reached out to these two so often for help, I am positive I would not be where I am today. Don't be shy to ask for help from people you admire. They've been through it before, sometimes through much worse. Successful people love to help others, I've found. There's something majorly fulfilling about passing on wisdom and guidance to a younger version of yourself.

> Keep working hard.
>
> Keep smiling a lot.
>
> Keep helping people out.
>
> Good things will always happen when you do those things. Don't waste time with negative energy people. Life is too short to invest even a second of our time with people who aren't willing to make us better.
>
> Have a great night!

The day I started Uptown, I reached out to Thomas to help me gameplan, only to find that he was out of town. He told me to take a pause, and he'd talk to me when he got back. "Slow down," he told me. "Don't do anything until we talk next week." *Well, too late.* When we touched base again a week later, he just laughed, realizing that I didn't slow down at all and, in fact, did quite the opposite. After he returned from his trip, he helped me refine my business model and offered all kinds of advice when I needed it, which was very often in the beginning. The one piece of his advice I refused to listen to was separating my sales and service team. I was not willing to budge on this. Other than that, Thomas's direction really helped me get everything moving the right way. I didn't know anything about laws, regulations, HR, or all that boring stuff you need to know. Being a fellow Texas business owner, he helped me finally get all my ducks in a row.

> **Don't be shy to ask for help from people you admire. They've been through it before, sometimes through much worse.**

A FINE DINING RESTAURANT

When first starting Uptown Marketing, I wanted to do a few things differently than Bloom, the biggest one being the role of a salesperson. Most good business owners, John and Thomas included, will preach the value of separating your sales team and your service team. Think about it: when you buy a car, sales and service are literally on two opposite ends of the building. That's intentional! However, I was passionate about wanting whoever sold a new client to also be the one providing the service on the account. This is what I did when I first started at Bloom, but as the company grew, I no longer had the option to do so. I could only keep a small number of accounts, and I had to pass on any new sales to my team. But the value of a business relationship is in just that: the relationship. I would build this great bond with an agent, learn about their office and their struggles, and then once I earned their trust, I had to . . . pass them on to *someone else*? I didn't like that! If someone decided to do business with us because of Samara, they would get to work with Samara the whole way through. I was *not* willing to compromise on this, even if it meant slower sales growth.

Uptown Marketing began to take root, processes were fine-tuned, and phones were ringing. As I settled into Dallas, I also settled into business ownership. I started dating a nice guy from New Jersey and focused on work. Dallas brought opportunities that Rochester didn't, one of which was how easily I could make connections. For instance, my spray tan artist introduced me to her photographer friend, who helped me brand my business in Dallas. Then, a few online magazines approached me and included my story in articles highlighting small business owners. From there, simply being known as a business owner in Dallas continued to lead to more opportunities, and my contacts led to appearances on podcasts about the insurance industry. All of this led to more clients coming our way.

In the early Wild West days of Uptown, I didn't treat the company like it solely belonged to me. No, it was a group effort between Samara, Mona, and me. We built the business together, which wasn't easy considering I lived in Texas while they still lived in New York. Communication in our little business looked like a whole lot of phone calls, FaceTimes, and text messages. Thank God for Mona because she wrote down everything I said while training them, whether that be over the phone or in person during the few times I flew them down to Texas. Over time, she translated all of her notes into one cohesive process. She found us all the right vendors for payroll and other operations. In other words, she took my ideas and turned them into a business. I told you: Mona instinctively complements my skills—I would've never even thought to document all of our conversations. I don't shut up long enough to do that.

Samara, as I've always known, is a natural with people. She signed the very first client she ever talked to. He actually ended up being a great client to have, especially at the beginning, because he referred a lot of business and was super supportive of our efforts. I'd met him before at a Bloom event, but he never became a client then. He loved everything we were doing at Uptown, and most of all, he was impressed with the way Samara handled his account. Samara bringing in clients meant that she felt motivated and rewarded, and it also took some pressure off of me. I wouldn't have to be the only one hustling for sales. I was so relieved to have her on the team.

Congrats
Today at 12:06 PM

Martina,

I just wanted to say congratulations on starting this new venture. I know it seems daunting to be on your own but I think that you will be awesome at what you are doing. Just wanted to tell you ▮▮▮▮ and I had a great convo, she is awesome. Really can tell she knows her stuff. Either that or she's the best BS'er in the game. Lol

I asked her how many agents yall had gotten so far and she said I made 8. Frankly a little upset I wasn't 1st. but hey, can't control timing.

I am excited to get in on the ground floor with yall and watch yall grow my marketing presence, as well as, watching yall grow as a company from scratch.... We share that same accomplishment/goal. I think you have done a great job at getting a good team In place and that makes a HUGE difference. Congrats again, and I am excited to work with you and everyone at Uptown Marketing.

I expect a Year anniversary get together in Dallas! Ill bring my dancing shoes. ;)

Training both her and Mona filled me with a lot of pride. It wasn't like my previous experience at Bloom where I trained the lead-gen reps how to read off of a script and get laughs over the phone. I had elevated the service. Training cold callers at Bloom was like teaching someone to work at McDonald's while training for Uptown was like teaching someone how to serve at a fine dining restaurant—no, how to *manage* a fine dining restaurant. I took so much more pride in it because I created it myself.

Over time, I continued to hire with intention. I was very particular about who could join the team. Brooke, a close friend of Samara's who can only be described as sunshine in human form, came next. A few months later, Ava, who left Bloom when we moved to Texas to work for an agent, was ready to come back to marketing. When it was time for more operational support, I looked to Maggie, an old friend of mine from back home in Rochester, and then my close friend in Dallas, a British blonde named Scarlett, followed after her.

I'd like to pause here and point out that if you're noticing the absence of male names on this list, it's not from a lack of trying. Three guys have worked for Uptown over the years, and each time, I learned again and again how vital it is for my team to be empathetic, detail-oriented, *and* motivated to the max. The traits that make you good at this job are traits more commonly found in women. I'm not saying that no man could ever succeed within our line of work, but I'll tell you this:

when you're building a new business, everything and everyone counts. I learned the same lesson three times in a row, and I'm not looking for a fourth anytime soon. There is no room for error, and the men who worked for me just didn't get that. (Though we did have a male intern who proved to be a great help to us, even with a broken collarbone.) I'd love to find the right guy to join the team permanently someday, but it hasn't happened yet. For now, we're the Uptown Girls. Sue me if you want, but remember who my lawyer is.

> **When you're building a new business, everything and everyone counts.**

PAJAMA PARTY

With this all-girl, absolutely stacked team, Uptown Marketing grew 400 percent in its first year. We grew so fast that we became an S corp. To celebrate our hard work, I took everyone to Miami for our one-year anniversary. We flew into Miami gossiping about the coronavirus, and we flew back home only hours before plane travel was banned. When you do work for an essential business, you become an essential business. We lost a total of one client due to COVID-related concerns. For everyone else, we buckled up and identified an opportunity. People were desperate to save money and had a lot of time on their hands to do tedious shit like shop insurance rates. We knew this and helped our clients lean in and be there when people were in need. My team already worked from home, so our day-to-day procedures barely changed. I recognized that I was extremely lucky my business was unaffected by COVID.

Like everyone during the COVID shutdowns, I went on a side quest. While most people were baking banana bread, I played matchmaker to an entire city. Here's what happened: during all the quarantine boredom, an idea struck me one day. I had two single girlfriends who struggled with dating, and I always wished I had a way to "wingman" for them on dating apps. So, I logged onto Facebook and started a dating group in Dallas, which I called "Dallas Wingman." I posted the rules: you could join this group if you were single and looking, or you could join as a wingman. Wingmen could post their single friends with all kinds of details, and other group members could comment if they were interested and strike up conversations via Facebook Messenger. I knew this was a great idea, but I had no idea how big it would get. Within weeks, there were over 4,000 members and a ton of activity. As soon as Texas deemed it safe, we hosted events where people could get together in person. And yes, the group worked. People were meeting, going on dates, starting relationships, and even simply making friends. My random idea connected thousands of people who were isolated during COVID and dying for connection. It was a fun, little place to focus all my pent-up energy and a great way to meet new people. Not even a pandemic could stop me from socializing.

It was even more fun later on when one of those single girlfriends whom I'd started the group for actually found the love of her life in Dallas Wingman.

Through this group, I was connected with a girl who asked me to be part of a new dating show on YouTube. Together with her and three other Dallas dating-scene podcasters, *The Pitch Dating Show* was born. We'd meet once a week in a studio to record live episodes where we'd have someone come on to "pitch" their single friend to the viewers. It was interactive too, so audience members could put in comments or questions throughout the episode. This show was so fun, but because it was no one's full-time job, eventually post-pandemic life took us all in different directions after a few months. You can still find it on YouTube—the pajama party episode is my favorite.

That summer, an influential Bloom client of Paul's named Andrew Armstrong slid into my Facebook DMs. I had helped Paul's assistant, Hannah, years ago by getting on a call with Andrew when Paul was out of the office. I barely remembered Andrew, but he remembered me enough to reach out when things weren't going so well for him anymore back at Bloom. His exact message? "Hey girl. I'm ready for your sales pitch."

Earning Andrew's business was surprisingly easy for what a huge deal it was. He gave tons of referrals at Bloom, and I mean *tons*. So, when he made a change to his marketing company, all of those people wanted to make a change too. It didn't hurt that Bloom was slipping pretty badly in my absence. We happily accepted all of Andrew's referrals and made sure to take great care of them. He's probably one of the most ideal clients anyone could ask for. Not only is he super laid back and funny, but he also has a side business where agents pay him to consult on their agencies. He's often asked to speak in different cities, and guess who was now invited to a lot of these networking events? We further strengthened our relationship with Andrew and even had our whole team fly out to an event of his in Florida. He continued to provide us with opportunities to meet new agents, and he sang the praises of our brand. A trusted resource among his peers, he kept sending agents in need of marketing help our way.

I'm making this all sound a little too easy, aren't I? Let me throw you a curveball then. Remember Campbell Enright, our Vegas king who kept us swamped with referrals? He was Paul's client, so when I left Bloom, I never tried to pursue his business. He was super supportive when I started Uptown though, and there was an open invitation to hang out if we found ourselves in Vegas.

So, you can imagine how much my heart sank when I heard rumors that Campbell Enright was getting involved in a new digital marketing company for insurance agents—one that would no doubt become Uptown's biggest competition.

Chapter 7

THE W HOTEL

"I don't believe in coincidences."

Yes, this one stung, but how could I not respect him for it? Campbell had been very engaged in his own marketing, knew a lot, and was obviously very well-connected and influential. It was an impressive move. I have no idea who officially owns this business, but Campbell's beautiful blonde girlfriend, Gracie, became the CEO and face of Digital Agent. When an agent was referred to Uptown who we couldn't take because his market was sold out, I referred the guy right to Gracie. She sent me a bottle of Dom Pérignon as a thank-you, and I decided I liked her. Establishing a good relationship with her was important to me—we had so many mutual connections, and I'm not the type to act like a brat over some fresh competition. Sure, in my ideal world, Campbell and all of his connections would be happy Uptown clients. But that's not the way this worked out.

As expected, there was a lot of hype around this new company, and we lost clients to them. I knew we would, but it still sucked when it happened. Most of the people who left had been referred to me by Campbell in the first place, so it only made sense they'd follow him where he went. His relationship with them beat mine. That can happen in business: you may have a great relationship with a client, but someone else out there has a stronger one. Some of the people I expected to lose, we didn't. I took comfort in the fact that *I* was the stronger relationship for so many of my clients, who were now being pursued more and more by other marketers. A few other companies that popped up were tied to agents or agents' relatives in some way. I guess certain agents saw the opportunity there and wanted to throw their hats in the ring too. I went from only competing with Bloom Industries and the corporate vendor to competing with eight or nine new companies that had formed to serve the exact same insurance agents I did.

But I knew I couldn't use this as an excuse for losing clients—competition always exists, but it's up to us to decide if we want to face up or lose face. I chose to work harder, identify more opportunities to network, and address our existing clients' needs before they even realized the need. We kept making appearances with Andrew or other various events, doing a great job at making new introductions. Sure enough, with time, things leveled out—Uptown gained a lot of new clients, and I found a friend in Gracie. It's more important to me to maintain good relationships than it is to squabble over a handful of clients. I respect them a lot; this industry is *not* easy. They grew a badass company in a short amount of time. It's actually been great to have Gracie to talk to; we understand each other. Like that scene at the end of *Bring It On* with the two opposing cheerleading captains.

I had to keep something in mind to continue growing my confidence: no other company would be *me*. I knew I had a leg up on all this new competition in the form of *years* of practice. I mean, by the time I started Uptown, I'd been helping insurance agents market their businesses for over 10 years if you go all the way back to my agency days. Present day, it's 15! All these new companies couldn't touch my experience. No other company had a Martina. Uptown's advantage was my industry knowledge, my passion for marketing, and my high standards for clients and myself. I couldn't forget that. I leaned into my expertise and my strong team, and I kept pushing ahead. Sometimes, you have to just stay in your lane and only focus on your own efforts. Remember what makes *you* great, over anyone else.

> **Competition always exists, but it's up to us to decide if we want to face up or lose face.**

HIGH RISK, HIGH REWARD

As happy as Dallas made me, the longer I was there, the more I missed home. I'd purchased my house in Texas during COVID, a beautiful ranch-style with an inground pool and hot tub. I actually put in an offer without even seeing it in person. I knew the real estate market was getting crazy competitive, and I wanted to own property in Texas. So, when my real estate agent sent me a video, I put in a competitive offer right away. I didn't want to miss the opportunity just because I was out of town. As much as I loved it, I once again felt like I had a house but not a home. My home was back in Rochester. My two sisters were my best friends, and I missed my mom and, of course, all of my girlfriends. After I left, watching them all go on with their lives got really hard. They'd FaceTime me when they were all together or send pictures, and my heart broke each time. Sometimes, I would question what I was even doing halfway across the country. *Was it worth being that far away?*

I almost reached the point of wanting to move home. But the nice guy from New Jersey I was still with (let's call him Ben) did not want to live in Rochester. My relationship with him became more and more serious (not to mention, messier), and I didn't have it in me to argue with him about it. Instead, I decided to look for a house in New York, so I could feel like I had a "second home" to stay in anytime I wanted to visit. I figured I could rent it out the rest of the time and make some money. My good friend is a realtor, so I asked her to find something small but nice. She sent me a few videos of a recently flipped house on the market, and I once again bought a house without ever stepping foot in it. My sister furnished it, and I listed it on Airbnb.

If there was one thing I wish Young Martina did more, it would be investing in real estate. When I sold my house in Rochester before I moved to Dallas, I was shocked at how much I made. Since then, I've been consulting with real estate agents and financial advisors to get better at investing. Buying that house in Rochester and turning it into an Airbnb was one investment that really made a difference. Of course, Airbnb has had its share of horror stories, but one thing to keep in mind is that it is high risk, high reward. Sure, some of the people who stayed at the house haven't exactly treated it with respect, but the investment paid off despite that. I filed an LLC to keep it all straight, and Martina Nicole Properties became official.

I realize that not everyone has the means to buy multiple houses, but guess what? The first house helps you get your second house, and so on. So, assess your options according to your needs, and don't use the excuse of being too young or it being too early in your career to invest. Do it. Trust me, your future self will thank both me and you for investing earlier. Investing doesn't have to mean real estate right now. Today's market does not favor first-time home buyers (or really, any home buyers), but there are programs to take advantage of. If you want it bad enough, you might be able to find a way to reprioritize your budget. Maybe start off with a small rental property instead of buying your dream home right away. This will lead to extra income, which might help you get an even better dream home.

Assess your options according to your needs, and don't use the excuse of being too young or it being too early in your career to invest. Your future self will thank you for investing earlier.

If real estate isn't the right fit for you now, set up an investment account. This is usually where you'll get the highest returns. If you prefer low risk, slow and steady, set up a life insurance policy that earns you money. I've heard Andrew Armstrong speak to a crowd about the benefits of these policies so often I feel like I could sell them myself. You know when old stockbrokers talk about "diversifying their portfolios"? All this means is spreading your investments out into different places. I have an investment account, 401k, an IRA, three pieces of real estate, and a whole life policy. Investments confuse the hell out of me, but I'm glad I finally started listening to the professionals. I have a financial advisor, a realtor, a CPA, and two insurance agents who have been super helpful in guiding me while I build my investment portfolio. Lean on the experts! But regardless of how you do it, make it happen. Even if it's $20 a month in an investment account, just do *something*.

EAT SOME PIZZA

Let's go back to 2020. Uptown is thriving. A guy named Felix VonBurton approached me to become part of an event he was hosting. I recognized his name—he was a business coach for agents, which was even more saturated than marketing. The best way to describe Felix is to say he was a complete schmoozer. He had the personality of a used car salesman, but somehow, he wasn't too off-putting. Once in a while, he would say or do something that made little alarms go off, but he was often nice to talk to, was supportive of our business, and seemed to get along great with my team. I'd heard bad things about him from people I trusted who called him "a scammer." So, I kept him at arm's length while exploring the opportunities he offered.

The event happened over a year later due to COVID. By the time I packed my girls up and headed to Nashville, it was September of 2021. I have to say: other than the drop off of over half his promised audience, it was a solid event and a fun trip. He made a real effort to build relationships with all of my team members, and spirits were high. We brought on a lot of new clients from this event, which meant I was almost starting to trust Felix. Almost.

On the other hand, my relationship with Ben was going downhill fast. We had moved in together, adopted dogs, gotten engaged, and done all the things I felt like I was supposed to be doing now that I was 30. But I couldn't stop the growing feeling that I was wearing a pair of shoes that didn't fit. The longer I wore them, the worse they felt. My stress and anxiety were through the roof, so I started therapy, hoping it would help me figure out my feelings. But no matter how hard I tried to force my life to look pretty and perfect on the outside, my relationship was falling apart at the seams, and I began to run out of excuses to tell myself. I started to get scary skinny from being in a constant state of stress. I grew up on Victoria Beckham and Kate Moss, so I didn't mind that part. But it was clear that my physical appearance was starting to reflect my mental state. In a really bad way.

One day, I woke up to the nastiest headache. I felt so bad that I had to go to an urgent care center, and then sure enough, they carted me off to the hospital. Turns out, I had almost no blood platelets. The doctors had me stay for a week, loaded me up with painkillers, and gave me blood transfusions and tons of tests. They found *no root cause*. My body was simply cracking under pressure. While it was no spa, it definitely gave me some time to take a breath. (If this doesn't tell us how far I'd been pushing myself for so long, I don't know what will.) Lying all day in the hospital, I had nothing to do except to look past the excuses and face the facts: I missed my family entirely too much; I felt intense pressure to make sure Uptown outperformed every single month and all the girls were happy; and the only person I had was Ben, who was starting to feel more like an enemy. This combo put my body in a flight-or-fight mode. I had reached a breaking point, and my body had given up.

After the Nashville event, my therapist suggested I take a break from Ben and Texas and go home to Rochester for a few weeks to see my friends and family. She specifically instructed me to "eat some pizza" and try to put on some weight. It lined up perfectly with another work trip I had scheduled, so it was decided: I'd go to Fort Lauderdale for a study group presentation with Samara and Scarlett, then head right home to Rochester.

Home felt like . . . *home*. I felt happier than I had in months. I used the opportunity to pick out a wedding dress with my sisters and friends (even though I secretly dreaded the thought of this wedding), ate great food, and caught up with them. I got to spend so much quality time with all my people that I started to feel like myself again. It was also a huge benefit to the business to be able to work in person with Mona, Brooke, and Maggie. We still worked from someone's dining room table, but as I've said, in-person work always beats virtual connection. Every time.

One of the things that I liked most about Bloom was having my team right beside me. Having an immersive workplace like that also made it a lot easier for my team members to hear how I talk with clients and learn from my conversations. It made training much more natural. Seeing someone every day also helps you gauge how they're feeling. Just one look can tell you if they're having a bad day, are in high spirits, or just want to be left alone. Being remote put up this barrier between me and the team, and no matter how hard I tried, I couldn't really "see" them beyond the screen. So, working with everyone in person felt like a fresh start, and it also re-opened my eyes to what Uptown was missing out on—I always knew, of course, but I had built up a wall of excuses for why I couldn't move back to Rochester and open an office space. Now, I questioned everything.

On October 1, 2021, I went out for a girl's dinner with my sisters, Mona, and Rosie. After dinner, someone suggested we go to a popular bar. Mona made us all laugh when she said, "We can go there, but one of us will probably run into an ex-boyfriend." And wouldn't you know, 15 minutes later, I was watching my first love, Aaron, walk through the door.

I feel like I should put a disclaimer here: the next part is a story just as corny as *The Notebook* or *Sweet Home Alabama*. It's dreamy and heartwarming for everyone involved—except James Marsden and Patrick Dempsey. Both were great guys who ended up getting the short end of the deal because the girl simply never got over her first love. The story starts out sweet, but there's some heartbreak in there before getting to the happily ever after.

GOOGLY-EYED

It took Aaron and me approximately three minutes to gravitate to each other and laugh our heads off like we were high school kids again. I'd heard through the grapevine he was recently divorced and had two cute little boys. He'd heard I was engaged and knew I lived in Texas and had started a business. We had the best time together, drinking and dancing and laughing like old times. I couldn't help but think how it had been so long since I had laughed that much. He kept half-joking that

I needed to move home—saying how I belonged here, with him.

Aaron *was* like home to me, in every way. Our connection is uncontrollable; we just truly get each other. It felt like yesterday that I'd dumped him at a Fourth of July party, but really, it had been a long eight years. I was distraught when we went our separate ways at the end of the night and a complete mess when I woke up the next day. I guess he was too because he sent me a message saying that he couldn't stop thinking about me and that he'd respect it if I asked him not to reach out again, but he had to see me. Unable to stop thinking about him either, I reluctantly agreed, convincing myself it was just as friends, though we had to go someplace no one would see us. If you don't believe in fate, listen to this: although we picked what we thought was the *last* place we'd be seen, someone we knew drove by and got a crystal-clear view of us looking at each other all googly-eyed, sipping mimosas together. The news didn't take long to get all the way back to Ben in Texas.

I'll spare the details since this isn't a romance novel, but just know that emotions were high. Within two weeks, I faced perhaps my biggest, most important life-altering decision. I was at a bachelorette party in Scottsdale. I had to decide whether to fly back to Texas to attempt to fix my severely damaged relationship with my fiancé or fly back to Rochester to roll the dice on a fresh start with my long-lost love. If it sounds dramatic, that's because it was.

When the rest of the girls left the trip, I stayed at the W Hotel for three days straight. I had no flight booked at all. I was paralyzed. For the first time in my life, I felt like I had to think through my next move carefully. I remember pausing and really trying to focus on picturing how my life would look if I went down each of the two different paths. I tried *so* hard to envision the two totally opposite lives. It was unfamiliar to me to analyze so much before making a decision. Deep down, I knew the answer the entire time; it was just going to be a tough move to make. It felt *insane* to throw away my entire life in Texas to move home and be with Aaron. But it felt even crazier not to.

If you take any lesson from this book, take this one. It's not about sales or business or marketing. It's about finding the courage to make a *really* tough, *really* selfish decision to change your life for the better. It's about doing what you know is right for you, even when it seems impossible. Stay completely true to yourself, even if you're hurting someone else in the process—because, if you don't, you'll hurt yourself even more. This decision, although it had nothing to do with business, was the single best decision I've ever made in my life. Of course, I felt guilty, but I never once regretted it. I've had some moments where I've literally cried over the thought that I almost let my life turn out completely different, and I would've missed out on my life with Aaron. This was a messy move, and I *know* people judged me for it at the time. But I don't care because it was the right move for me. If I felt any tiny bit of shame, it was all worth it to me in the end. I'd go back and do it again, a million times over.

> **Stay completely true to yourself, even if you're hurting someone else in the process—because, if you don't, you'll hurt yourself even more.**

After taking my flight from Scottsdale to Rochester, I started the process of my cross-country move. I bought a house and made plans to remodel the whole thing. I had to be back in Dallas to be a bridesmaid in a wedding a few weeks later. (Yes, the Dallas Wingman couple was now getting married!) The morning after the wedding, I went back to my house and packed up my car as much as I could, left my engagement ring on the counter, and told my dogs I'd see them soon. Aaron flew down to Dallas to drive my car back, bringing me home with him for good.

I've heard so many people justify staying in bad relationships because they have a house together, or are raising dogs, or whatever the excuse is. Houses can be sold, and pets are very adaptable as long as they're loved. Most of the excuses are just logistics, and logistics are easily figured out. There's a solution to everything. Do not let anything get in the way of going after what you want. Have you ever had to make a huge decision like this, one that you knew would completely alter the course of your life? How about a decision that you knew you'd be judged for? Did you make the right decision? It's not easy, but it's so worth it to follow your heart.

Okay, enough of the mush. Let's get back to business. You made it to the home stretch.

Chapter 8

PHOENIX

"You have two ears and one mouth; listen twice as much as you speak."

I'd be a big liar if I said that once I was home, I gave Uptown everything I had. In reality, I was in a happy, little bubble and didn't feel like dealing with anything outside of love, fun, and home. I now lived in the same town as three of my employees, but three others were still scattered across the country. On top of that, the industry kept changing—a lot of marketing companies that "specialized in insurance agents" kept popping up, and the Internet had been evolving at a crazy speed, making digital marketing a whole new ballgame. COVID put online shopping into overdrive, which meant that more businesses wanted a piece, our clients had to spend more, and the Uptown Girls and I would have to work harder to get the same, let alone better, results for our clients as we did the previous year. These new challenges pushed my team harder than ever, and at a time when they needed me most, I was acting like that meme of Elizabeth Taylor lounging in bed, wearing silk feathery pajamas.

Despite being in my chill season, I, of course, couldn't completely shut off my brain from my business. I'd discovered a new asset that could help me tighten up Uptown: Aaron. He's a really smart guy in general, and he'd found success in software sales. He knows a lot about data, automation, and all the technology stuff that I hate. It baffled him that I'd somehow built an entire seven-figure business using Google Sheets and the bare minimum of software systems. But in the beginning, I didn't care about using specialized programs—I wanted to keep moving forward, not spend hours researching software. Now, I can acknowledge that the right systems will help me move forward more efficiently. I have to admit: it's pretty nice to have Aaron help me get my technological shit together. (Don't tell him I said that.) We completely revamped our software systems, and Mona built new, rock-solid workflow processes. I could write an entire book on my thoughts about the future of automation versus the classic, old-school ways of business, but I won't. I can be stubborn about not letting technology handle too many things, but I've started to understand the value at times.

CIRCUS ACTS

During all of this, Felix VonBurton continued inviting us to events, and while they benefited our sales, he also started to take a weird leadership role with my girls. He started a group text with my entire team and sent words of encouragement every morning, which started to feel sleazy and confusing. Why was he putting so much time into us? At one point, he privately asked me if I wanted to "own a part of his business." I told him I was happy to partner on events, but I would not formally or financially involve myself with another vendor like that. I felt super weirded out after that phone call and thought of the multiple warnings I'd heard about Felix, especially the "scammer" comment.

Felix also wanted me to use my connections, like my long-time friendship with crowd-pleaser Andrew Armstrong, and get them involved in his latest and greatest project. He kept promising these grandiose gestures and then would be unreachable for days. It felt off. But the invitations to events kept coming, and they were profitable every single time. I thought that as long as I kept a safe distance and the events remained good for business, everything would be fine. *It's fine, I'm fine, everything's fine.*

You know when you go on a really long, adventurous vacation, and then you finally get home and just want to relax and decompress? That's how I felt at this time. I was so over getting on a plane, doing a conference, and then hopping right back on a plane home. Forget traveling; I wanted to stay home, relax, and spend time with all my friends and family who I'd missed so much. I mean, I used to fly all over the country, often by myself, when I worked at Bloom, so I thought, "Why can't the girls go pick up some business on their own?" So, I sent them to multiple cities for these events: Atlanta and Chicago, to name a few. And during each one of these trips, they all spent a ton of off-the-record time with Felix.

I'll be the first to admit that I was too disconnected from Uptown during this time. If I had been a little more hands-on, I may have predicted what came next. But looking back, I have to cut myself a little slack. The happy chaos going on outside of work took priority. The renovations on my new house consumed a lot of my time and caused major decision fatigue. All of my belongings from Texas sat in boxes in my garage, and I stayed at Aaron's in the meantime with my dogs who finally made the cross-country trip home to me. I literally lived out of bags for months. I was so thrilled to be there that it didn't even bother me. I felt like a carefree minimalist.

As if that wasn't enough, I decided to purchase a third house to turn into another Airbnb property, which needed to be fully furnished and decorated. Was this really the best time for an investment property? While most people would say *hell no*, my answer would be yes. Despite all the insanity, I had money to invest, and I'd already identified an opportunity to make extra cash from my first Airbnb property. Once it proved profitable, I figured it would be a no-brainer to buy and manage another one. The market wasn't getting any better, and I'd always said my one regret was not investing more money earlier in life. So, I put a lot on my plate between these two houses, which meant less energy to focus on work.

Juggling is a circus act for a reason—it's not easy, and not everyone can do it. The ability to handle multiple projects at once is a skill that you can and should always improve on. The key to this is empowering key players to delegate certain tasks. For example, my mom took over as "property manager" for both my Airbnbs and did a lot of the work I didn't have time to do. It's impossible to run multiple businesses yourself. I swear some of the best business owners are just amazing delegators.

Speaking of delegating, I'd been begging my big sister, Alexis, to work at Uptown for years, and finally, the timing was right. She came on as the vice president of business development and took a huge burden off my shoulders: managing and training the sales team. She also took over conferences and events. In the areas where I failed as a leader, Alexis picked up the slack as an amazing manager. And I needed her badly; I was finding it harder and harder to guide Samara, Brooke, and Scarlett, who always seemed stressed and burnt out no matter what solutions I offered. When I tried to help, I felt pushback, and because I was so lost at how to discover what the *real* problems were, I fired back with emotional responses. This was not a time when my emotions helped me, especially the few times I ended meetings early in tears of frustration. Can you imagine your boss hanging up on you during a Zoom call in tears? But before Alexis could swoop in and save Uptown by providing the girls with much-needed guidance, *someone else* had already weaseled his way into being the solution.

The ability to handle multiple projects at once is a skill that you can and should always improve on.

On May 11, 2022, I had three separate phone conversations with Scarlett, then Samara, and then Brooke. All of the calls ended with them leaving Uptown Marketing and loose comments about going to work for Felix. I was devastated. Losing Samara hit me hard—she was my day-one Uptown Girl. They were unhappy with their jobs because I had failed to provide them with the right environment for growth and fulfillment. I felt like I let my girls down, and that was the worst feeling in the world. My leadership style did not benefit them, so they looked to Felix to find something I wasn't providing: mentorship. I tried my best to give them the same level of guidance, but you have to remember that I'm friends with all of these girls. Have you ever tried to train a friend to do something? When you're close enough to someone, they'll usually have no trouble communicating when they're annoyed. Having difficult conversations with them about performance and procedures always sucked and, more often than not, resulted in someone crying. I was the mean parent who kept telling my kids to do their chores, and Felix was some random uncle who came out of the woodwork and could pop in and promise excitement without taking any real responsibility for them.

 I'll never know what conversations happened between Felix and the girls or what he offered during the events I didn't attend. But in typical Felix fashion, he promised them exorbitant salaries and C-suite-level titles. Only a few short months later, I found out that not only did he *not* fulfill his promises to the girls, but he also began to screw them over little by little. Luckily, he ended up losing all of them to better opportunities. As much as the whole situation sucked, I'm so happy the girls moved onward and upward. I'm glad they're all now in roles at great companies where they are valued and treated with the respect they deserve. I stopped answering Felix's pathetic, desperate messages to try to stay on good terms with me. I will never align myself with him again nor will I be shy to spread this story to anyone in our industry. People deserve to know who they're dealing with.

SILVER BULLET

After May 11, the girls quitting left me in mental shambles: I was depressed, crying, and overwhelmed. It seemed like the world ended overnight. But I didn't have time to grieve for long; Uptown was in one hell of a pickle. More than *200 clients* no longer had an account manager. Ava, the only person left in sales, had the most clients out of anybody, so I couldn't expect her to manage 200 extras, though she did browse through the list and take a few she wanted. The rest of the accounts were up to Alexis, who had been with Uptown for a month at that point, and me to split down the middle. I'm grateful that most of the clients were super understanding, patient, and even sympathetic as a lot of them had been in similar situations in their own businesses. A small number of them did cancel their contracts as they had grown attached to their previous account managers and didn't want to change.

After letting me have a short (but dramatic) meltdown, Alexis and Mona confronted me: if I wanted any chance of surviving this loss, we had to move forward with hiring. Our first three interviews ended with incredible new hires, all of whom are still with Uptown, and after a scary couple of months, I felt like I could breathe again . . . but something was still missing. I needed a silver bullet.

Remember Hannah, who I'd saved from the chopping block by getting Paul to hire her as his assistant? She was somehow still stuck in the muck at Bloom. I mean, even Paul had moved on by that point to start his own company. But Hannah was loyal, hardworking, and never complained—she got the job done. Her clients loved her.

One day, I sent Hannah a text and asked her if she wanted to grab dinner. Over wine and filet mignon, she confirmed all of my suspicions: she was very unhappy at Bloom. Not only was she not being valued as the most tenured person left on the insurance team, but they had actually changed her pay structure, resulting in a salary decrease even though she had taken on *more* clients. After learning that, any and all guilt vanished. Alexis had commented that recruiting Hannah could "start a war" with Bloom, but I didn't care. Many people wouldn't make the same decision, seeing it as overstepping a boundary, but from my perspective, I was the one who brought Hannah into the insurance department all those years ago. I saw her potential when she was days away from being let go. I helped train her at Bloom, and I invested my time in her development. More importantly, I knew she deserved a better opportunity. After a week of meetings and mulling it over, Hannah became an Uptown Girl.

I felt like I had drafted a star quarterback to my team. Hannah didn't need any training; she could jump in on her first day and go, go, go. I knew this move would put Uptown in a position to win. It was ballsy of me, but all that ended up happening was a friendly reminder from the Bloom attorney that she couldn't seek out Bloom clients. It wasn't a problem at all because, once people saw on social media that Hannah was an Uptown Girl, her old clients came running. To this day, people still switch to Uptown because they love Hannah and want to work with her.

The day Hannah started was also the first day in our new office space. Finally, I had the whole team together in person again. My immersive training method was back in action. Simply by sitting near Hannah, Mona, and Maggie, our new team members learned so much. My intuition had been nagging at me for years that getting the whole team into an office in person would solve so many communication and training problems, and I was right. The girls left to join Felix in May, Hannah's first day was at the beginning of July, and by September, we had exceeded our previous number of clients and continued beating our growth objectives once again. Like a phoenix, we rose from the ashes.

The lesson I learned from all of this is that it's possible to be *too good* at networking, to the point where you get involved with people who you shouldn't. The school of hard knocks taught me this again when I had trouble with my CPA firm, which was made up of insurance industry friends who had worked with me on several events over the years. I'd known them since my days at Bloom, and they handled all my books when I started Uptown. We had a great relationship. So, it kinda sucked when, after four years, the owner called to tell me that not only had they made a massive, expensive mistake on my taxes, but they were also starting a competing marketing company—after having access to my client list, vendors, and backend business operations for years. The hard part of becoming emotionally invested in business relationships is that people will let you down. You can't expect everyone to operate with the same level of integrity that you do. You can only uphold your own morals and hope others will follow suit. And most will. It's the ones who don't that really burn. But we haven't lost one client to them.

> **You can't expect everyone to operate with the same level of integrity that you do. You can only uphold your own morals and hope others will follow suit.**

NOTHING ON THE SIDE

When I think of founding Uptown Marketing, I'm most proud of how integrity is built into its core foundation. Many companies have entered our space over the years, but we're one of the only ones that offers market exclusivity, meaning none of my clients can market in the same zip code. While I could have easily grown the business more by taking on any and all clients, no matter where they're located, I have never been afraid to turn clients away if it means providing a more valuable service to my current accounts. After all, our clients come to us for a personal touch and high standards, not because we're the biggest player on the field. That reputation is important to me.

The fact is, you can't have successful and effective marketing tactics if you have multiple clients in the same area who are all trying to capture the same audience. At its core, marketing is all about differentiating a business. How can an agent stand out if all of their competitors have an identical strategy, provided by the same marketing company? I wouldn't be able to take pride in my work if I tried to market a bunch of agents in the same area. It defeats the purpose of doing marketing to begin with. Without maintaining market exclusivity, it's impossible to do my job with authenticity. And as a true marketing girl, I was not going to compromise on that.

In addition to this fundamental policy, I'm also grateful that I can say Uptown was not founded by an insurance agent or a CPA firm that started a marketing company on the side. For us, there's nothing "on the side" about it. I have always loved marketing, and it has been my passion for decades. This is my entire career, and I'd have it no other way. It also helps that everyone at Uptown is just *really good at it*.

Marketing has always been, and always will be, the center of our business. And we will continue to do it as transparently and sincerely as we can. I believe that this has been the key to our success (in addition to our strong relationships, of course). My industry is one where it's incredibly easy to backslide, yet Uptown never has, even with more and more competition coming in. Even through all that nonsense with Felix and, yes, my poor management skills (I never said I was perfect!), I'm so appreciative that Uptown has continued to grow every single year without fail. As some companies pop up and become all the rage only to fizzle out, Uptown remains strong and steady, not going anywhere any time soon.

The secret to this? Set high standards for yourself, your team, and your environment. Know what makes you the most proud about your business. Let that bring you confidence when the highs and lows bring you down. And don't ever sacrifice it.

Ready for the last chapter?

Chapter 9

CEO

"Keep working hard. Keep smiling a lot. Keep helping people."

Toward the end of the chaos in 2022, life started to settle. Well, sort of. I mean, I did start a brand new division of Uptown. An idea came to me, and I ran with it.

When a new employee starts at Uptown Marketing, she is given custom-branded Uptown merchandise. I'm not talking about a polo shirt with a tiny logo on the pocket or a mug with our name on it. Our merch is unique, modern, and stylish. We've done everything from cropped hoodies to sneakers, from denim jackets to bucket hats, and we keep finding ways to make our merch stand out. I *was* voted Best Dressed in high school, after all. I loved having Uptown gear that was actually cool. And then I started thinking. . .

If I loved this for my own business, wouldn't our clients love it for theirs? Agents want their logos printed on *everything*. But what if we made a product that would not only help with their individual branding but also boost interaction for their social media, website, and business? We officially started offering custom-branded merchandise to all of our clients in September of 2022. We help design logos and pick out custom looks for the agents and their team members, family, friends, and community. We even print QR codes on the sleeves of sweatshirts that lead right to their website. They can have any social media handles on there too. I called it "Street Marketing," a little play on Uptown. Executing all of this was a huge learning curve, but I was ready to jump into something new.

Was it easy and seamless? Hell no! But we made it happen, mistakes and all. It's proven to be a risk worth taking—and helped my business continue to grow and provide additional value to our clients.

There is a certain irony in business ownership. I left Bloom because I wanted more control. I was tired of answering to people, had so many ideas I wanted to run freely with, and was over being treated like the rebellious little sister. But after almost five years in full control, I've realized the major thing that changed my business and my life for the better is *letting go of control*.

My big ego says I always know the right answer, and I'm the best at getting it done. So, why would I let go? *Because it's impossible to stay sane if I don't.* When I was in my 20s with endless energy and no responsibilities, it made sense for me to throw 150 percent of my focus into work. I'm glad I did it when I could—it clearly paid off. But now, I have a husband, stepsons, dogs, family, and friends who I moved back to Rochester to live life with. Having the support of Alexis and Mona and a really reliable team made a huge difference in my stress levels. It made it possible for me to play in real estate and take vacations that don't involve conferences or presentations. If there's one thing I've grown to appreciate, it's that I've learned how much I'm willing to trade control for time. Time to breathe, to make memories, and to make other big, bold moves that sound fun.

Uptown has landed in an amazing place. There is still a lot about the way I run my business that goes against the grain, and I believe strongly in all of it.

SEXY, SMART

Let's talk a little about the team. First of all, none of what I'm about to share applies to you unless you have the right team in place. Hiring and retaining the right people is *not* easy—if you've ever had to recruit for a position, you know how painful it can be. One trick that's served me well is looking right past the "qualifications." I truly couldn't care less about a resume when hiring. I hire on personality. I look for confidence, attention to detail, and ambition. As long as a candidate has the right attitude, we can teach the rest.

Another important element to consider is how a candidate will respond to your leadership style, especially if you're a small-sized company. I need people who can operate independently and are self-motivators. Identifying your own leadership style and the style of your management team is the only way to ensure you're putting the right players in position. I've learned that people who require a lot of hand-holding don't find fulfillment at Uptown. There's *nothing* wrong with you if you do. It's just incompatible with my leadership style. I can't spend tons of time training and micromanaging; I lead by example. Alexis handles all the accountability processes—she makes sure we communicate expectations clearly through weekly team meetings, quarterly reviews, and goals.

Our office culture is everything we are: hard-working but still laidback and fun. In the area where the team sits, there's a black statement wall with an Uptown Marketing sign on it. We have photography art all over—from a huge Dallas skyline, to a big, black vintage rotary phone, to a picture of women protesting and holding up signs that say, "Protect the mini-skirt." The private offices where Alexis, Mona, and I sit are painted hot pink. It definitely keeps us alert. There's no dress code because I really don't care what you wear to work. If you're getting results, I don't care if you're in a sweatshirt and slippers or in a blazer and heels.

I don't care if a team member clocks in an hour late with a little hangover nor do I care if someone leaves early to take their dog to the vet. They have no limit on vacation or sick days and a loose start time. I can offer all of this because when you give the right people this freedom, no one ever takes advantage. The real questions are: are their clients happy? Do they work well with their teammates? Do they complete tasks on time? Just because my team is allowed to come to work in yoga pants doesn't mean we don't have high standards. My team recognizes that I'm not the *least* bit laid back when it comes to results and our clients' satisfaction, and they take it just as seriously. This is so overplayed, but our culture really is to work hard, play hard. I don't take excuses when it comes to work, but I use every excuse to make sure the girls are having a good time. I want them to enjoy their jobs and feel fulfilled, just like I do every day. Is every day perfect? No, but it's usually nothing we can't fix by laying blankets on the office floor, sitting down together, and having a picnic or a glass of champagne.

Letting go of control also means that I can focus on what I love most: being the marketing girl. I find the greatest joy in working with clients directly and working on our own brand. When we first started Uptown, Mona, Samara, and I always called our brand "sexy, smart." I used to get a hard time from Helen and other boring people who were worried about how I'd come across to people by looking a certain way. But we wanted to be free to be ourselves. We've shown you can be the hot girl wearing heels, and you can also be smart as hell and the best at what you do. Did we ever intend for the Uptown brand to grow into this all-female powerhouse? Definitely not, especially since I don't vibe with the condescending "girl boss" mentality.

But that's what I mean when I say branding should, above all else, be authentic. What you see is what you get. Our brand grew alongside the actual culture of the business. I love style, and I love an awesome photoshoot. I wear makeup and have long hair extensions, and that doesn't make me any less smart. And if my whole team just happens to be hot girls, then there's nothing I can (or want to) do about that. When our clients give me feedback, the words they use to describe our team are things like "She's always on point," or "She's been so helpful for my office." As great as our photo shoots turn out, I'm the most confident in who my team members are on the inside. No one can top their brains and work ethic.

Another very rewarding practice of ours is giving back. For years now, we've volunteered tons of time, money, and resources to organizations that help different communities. Our favorite is Girls on the Run, a non-profit dedicated to empowering young girls through physical, mental, and social exercises. Our whole team comes together twice a year to support the cause, and it's one of my favorite times of the year: I get to see how generous and caring my team is. Specifically Alexis, who makes sure we all participate and donates tons of her time to be a board member. I very much recommend getting involved in an organization you're passionate about. There is no better feeling than giving back.

As my industry becomes more competitive and saturated, I continue finding ways for us to stand out. We recently started a podcast that has already proven to bring in new clients while giving our audience a chance to get to know us beyond the pictures on our website. My brand should reflect my marketing skills—if I'm able to establish us as a put-together, eye-catching, and intelligent company, shouldn't I be able to do the same for my clients? How can my clients trust me to capture the essence of their brands if I'm not even able to perfect my own? So, my top priority is to always make sure Uptown's personality is reflected in every move we make as a company and in every piece of marketing that is sent out to the world.

Authenticity is not easy. It can be intimidating to put your true self out there for the world to judge. But when brands embrace it and do themselves justice, they attract clients who are the right fit. Not every insurance agent should be an Uptown Marketing client. We have a certain business model, processes we follow, and a personality about us that is not the right fit for everyone. We don't fall into the trap of making guarantees we can't back up just to earn a client. We're transparent and realistic. We are results-focused, but we are relationship builders at heart. We're just *ourselves*.

NOT PERFECT

I've realized there are struggles that I will always have as a business owner. It can be incredibly isolating. I know I keep encouraging you to take risks, but I mean to take risks that will achieve *your* version of success. Business ownership is not for everyone. The responsibility shifts from only being responsible for yourself to being responsible for an entire company. That means yourself, the business as a whole, all of your employees, and all of your clients. It sometimes gives me *physical* anxiety.

If you're like me and thrive on praise, good luck as the owner. I really miss the Bloom days when, every morning, the whole company got an email with sales numbers that basically said, "Martina is the best salesperson here!" I miss the intense sales meetings, the whiteboard that ranked everybody, and being presented with big, shiny trophies at company parties. When I started Uptown, I lost all of this. I learned how much I really value it all from my time there.

My recognition now comes in less obvious ways. When I'm asked to speak at a conference or on a podcast, that's a great ego boost. I'm given a lot of praise by our clients, which means the world to me. Now that I'm the owner of their marketing company and not just their sales rep, they look at me as a peer. There's no better feeling than when someone I respect tells me how much they respect *me* and what I've built. An even better feeling? When they ask *me* for advice.

Another struggle I'll always have is anything operational or structural. I've said many times how much I value Alexis and Mona—and they deserve every single bit of praise. Alexis has done an amazing job taking over travel and networking. A huge lesson I learned in leaving Bloom was that I *can't* do it all by myself. I need partners who are strong where I'm weak. They never fail to take my ideas and turn them into reality. It's much more fun to run a business with your sisters. They lead this strong team that I can trust to deliver the best experience to all of our clients.

See? I'm not perfect. I'm far from it! But one thing I'm good at is never questioning myself. I hope you can learn to do this too.

Getting to where I am today has not been easy. As a business owner, your job is never done, and that gets exhausting. I lose sleep thinking about my clients and employees. In sales, it's always, "What have you done for me lately?" Owning a business is no different. You can't think about your successes from yesterday because it's over. You can only make sure the lessons you learned *yesterday* can help your *tomorrow* be even more successful. I've done a great job so far, but what will I do next? I might not know the outcome, but I know it will be good. The best way to know for sure that good things will happen is to *make* them happen.

This doesn't only apply to marketing, sales, and business but to every aspect of life. As I've been saying, truly getting to know yourself is the only way to learn how to become the best version of yourself. Learning your own strengths and weaknesses can help you prioritize where you put your energy. Focusing on your strengths instead of your weaknesses will give you so much more confidence and purpose in life. Becoming a more sure version of yourself is the best way to put all the advice and insights in this book into practice and take risks you would have previously shied away from.

> **You can only make sure the lessons you learned *yesterday* can help your *tomorrow* be even more successful.**

What are my goals for the next five to 10 years? C'mon, you know me by now. I don't set goals. I don't think about the finish line. I just run. But as I look forward, I see a future of fun, big, crazy moves. I see learning and growth. I see lots of marketing. Most importantly, I see happiness, love, and success. I don't know what this looks like, but I know it's there and I know I can get it. Of course, this won't be easy; nothing has been easy in my life so far. So, I'll use what I have in my arsenal—self-confidence, passion, and the ability to bet on myself. What's in your arsenal? Identify your strongest weapons and use them.

I know you're about to head out on a similar path yourself, so it's time to get movin'. Do what you want. Stop worrying about what other people think. It doesn't have to be perfect. I hope I've shown how you can find success while also being a human (and even a hot mess sometimes). It doesn't have to be a drastic leap—a small step still takes you forward. No more doubting yourself; you can take action exactly as you are. Turn your fear into excitement. Go make it happen.

The best way to know for sure that good things will happen is to *make* them happen.

Afterword

I've always wanted to write a book. I loved reading growing up—I used to hide books under my pillow and read when I was supposed to be going to sleep. When my sisters would put a movie on, I'd lay on the floor with a book while it played. What a nerd!

The reason I wrote *this* book is because I've noticed myself having the same conversation with so many people over the years. In fact, it happened only two days ago at a bar. Aaron and I went to watch a football game with another couple, and once the topic of work and jobs got brought up, I found myself in very familiar territory.

It starts with asking about my business: "Wait, how many employees do you have? Are they actually W-2?" I get this one a lot as if it's unfathomable that I could afford real payroll for a team of 12. You should see their faces when I tell them there are full benefits, including 401k and unlimited time off. Then, it goes into some version of, "But how did you *do* that?" And it brings me all the way back to the beginning of this story.

The questions might vary, but the tone of the conversation is always the same. Disbelief and confusion. I remember a college friend once resurfaced in my Instagram DMs and asked me for career advice. At the end of her message, she said, "I guess I just don't understand how you're doing what you're doing." Maybe the skepticism comes from the fact that I'm pretty young or because I don't come across as someone super serious and disciplined. I'm a very average 32-year-old girl. Ugh, I mean woman. I don't have family money or high-profile connections. I have no investors and no business partners. I live in a very mundane suburb in Upstate New York. I'm not your stereotypical CEO by any means.

What I want this book to teach you is that *there is no secret to success*. Success is found exactly where they always told us it would be—by working hard, treating people right, and taking chances.

When dreaming of next steps, people convince themselves that they have to wait. Wait until they have some kind of skill or certification; wait until they have a certain amount of money; or even just wait until they magically feel *ready* to make a big move. Usually, none of those barriers are *actually* holding them back. The real obstacles are insecurity, self-doubt, and a lack of confidence. As long as you can identify what your ideal life looks like, the only thing stopping you from going after it is . . . you.

There will be a solution to every problem you face; you just have to go find it. Have faith in yourself to do it the right way, and even if you do screw up, trust yourself to find a way to fix it. Do I have to say it again? Take action. Figure out the rest later.

There is no secret to success.

It doesn't mean it's going to come without struggle. You just read years worth of challenges a person went through to achieve something. I've had so many moments of, "Oh shit, what do I do now?" I'm an empathetic person who cares a lot for the people around me. My actions have hurt people before, which has emotionally weighed on me. People have also hurt me before, which has caused serious grief too. I have weaknesses, especially when it comes to management, patience, and side note, anything domestic. But because I'm able to focus on my strengths, I see outcomes for myself that don't involve fear. I don't fret over decisions and ask myself, "What happens if it doesn't work out? What could go wrong?" Any time you gamble, you take a risk. You're way more likely to hit the jackpot when you ask, "What could happen if it goes *right*?"

One of my girlfriends has a philosophy that I love: *make a decision, and then make that the "right" decision.* If you choose to stay in a relationship you debated ending, then that's great. You better work your ass off to make that the right decision for you. If you choose to start a business, even better. Work around all of the obstacles until that becomes the right decision. And if you choose to buy a house, then keep making decisions in order to pay for that house: pick up extra shifts, select the right loan, or find a better-paying job. Make the big decision that will make you happy, and then force it to work. Think of the positive outcomes, and whatever you do, never question yourself, change your mind, or back out. Not when you're taking steps to change your life for the better.

Remember that any decision you make can probably be un-made. Take my own story, for example. I moved across the country to Dallas on a whim. I was so sure of it. That decision left me lonely and stressed out, but I wouldn't ever call it the wrong choice because it brought me to where I am today. When I knew that Dallas wasn't working out, I undid my previous decision. Two and a half years after moving, I went crawling back to Rochester with my tail between my legs, and I didn't regret it one bit. That's what I wanted to do, so I did it. And that's what I mean: there's a solution for everything. If you make a shitty decision, make *another* decision to fix it. Keep making decisions until you create the life you want.

Make a decision, and then make that the "right" decision.

I'm not an analytical person by any means, so I understand data-driven people need different decision-making processes from mine. All I'm encouraging these people to do is write up a "pros" and "cons" list. Then, cross out all of the "cons." Simple!

Focus on your personal "pros" column. Make a list of five strengths that you're better at than anyone else. My little sister, for example, knows more about dogs than anyone else I know. She fosters and rescues them, volunteers her time and resources, and makes all these amazing, selfless moves. My best friend, as another example, is the best mom in the world. She can bake and do home renovations—she's the domestic goddess I could only dream of being. I envy both of them; I lack everything they have. I have lots of flaws and insecurities. But what am I going to do about it? Let my imperfections beat me down? No way. Every person has a ton of strengths. When you only focus on the things you can't do, you'll feel like a loser. But when you center yourself around what you do the best and what brings you the most joy, then you'll always be feeling great about yourself and doing what you love.

    I want to make it clear how thankful I am for Bloom Industries. I'm thankful for Nick, of course, but also for Tony and Helen and even Paul. It was the start of my career and taught me so much about myself and what I'm good at. I learned everything there. Good and bad. I'm so appreciative of Mona and Alexis who, no matter what happens in this business, always have my back. They will always be there with me, and I can always trust them. My whole team too: I'm *sooo* lucky to have such hard-working and caring women beside me. The phone calls, endless advice, and much-needed reassurance from my mentors, John and Thomas, also can't be forgotten. I don't know how I would've kept going without them there to hear me out and keep me on the right track. And Aaron, still my favorite person, is a constant reminder that following your heart is *always* the right decision.

Thank you, reader, for picking up this book and reading my story. I'm grateful for you too. I hope that if you've gained anything from this, it's that success is here for you if you want it. You'll have to make some big moves to get where you want to go. The ups and downs aren't optional. Don't overthink it. I've achieved so much without following any plan or structure. I flew by the seat of my pants, and you can do the same, as long as you start flying in the first place.

Anything you've been talking yourself out of doing—go do it. Or at least take the first step. Buy a plane ticket. Double-text your crush. Adopt a dog. Quit your job. Go on vacation. Dump your boyfriend. Do none of those. Or do all of those, if you're really feeling it.

I can't wait to see where it takes you.

Acknowledgments

To my best friend and husband, Aaron: thank you for loving the 17-year-old me and the 32-year-old me all the same. Life has changed, but we certainly have not. You are the most fun part of every day. You didn't blink an eye when I told you I was writing a book. How cool that I discovered the two greatest loves of my life in the same room: you and marketing.

To my right hand and my left hand, Alexis and Mona: your high standards and dedication to Uptown have given me the ability to sleep at night. There are no two people who have been there for me through my entire crazy life the way you two have. I can't put my love and gratitude into words. I remember sitting at Mom's kitchen table making a Ti Amo 2 business plan together—I'm still down if you guys are.

Samara, you were the first person to give me the idea to start a business and the confidence to make it happen. You gave up a solid career to follow me into the unknown, and you'll never know how much courage that gave me. You are so special to me!

To John Romano, my first client of my own and someone I now consider family: you never once doubted me, and you helped me grow my business not once but twice. Thank you for your loyalty, friendship, and laughs.

You are truly the big brother I never wanted and my ride-or-die client forever. Whether you like it or not.

Thomas Hebert, thank you for being the leader I needed when I didn't have one. Thank you for answering every question and always making time, giving me all the advice, and helping me understand my strengths and weaknesses. You took valuable time to turn the marketing girl into a stronger, better version of herself from halfway across the country. I'm lucky to have you as a mentor, and I'm proud to be a younger, dumber version of you.

To Andrew Armstrong, the guy who slid into my DMs and has been a loyal friend and client ever since: I know you love AB more than me, but our bond is still really special. I can't thank you enough for writing the foreword to this book without hesitation. It just goes to show how big your ego really is.

To every Uptown Girl, past and present: I love each and every one of you so much and can't thank you enough for everything you've done for me. We've been through a lot together, and you are all sisters forever. You should be extremely proud of who you are. I know I'm proud of you.

Nick, you were the best boss I've ever had. So much of what I live by was learned from you back in those early days. Your energy and leadership style is unmatched—you change lives. Thank you for encouraging me to run.

Kimmy, you are the greatest little sister ever and an amazing sounding board. You were the first person I shared this book with, which was a no-brainer. Thank you for always being there for me and giving me many words of affirmation.

My mom and dad gave me the best of both of them. Thank you, Mom, for your personality, authenticity, warmth, and humor. Thank you to my dad for my high standards, integrity, and nonstop work ethic.

Helen—thank you for sending me that text.

Notes

1. "One third of your life is spent at work," Gettysburg College, accessed December 1, 2023, https://www.gettysburg.edu/news/stories?id=79db7b34-630c-4f49-ad32-4ab9ea48e72b.

2. Kimberly Holland, "Amygdala Hijack: When Emotion Takes Over," last modified March 16, 2023, https://www.healthline.com/health/stress/amygdala-hijack.

3. *The Real Housewives of New York City*, season 10, episode 4, "War and P.O.S.," featuring Dorinda Medley, Sonja Morgan, and Ramona Singer, aired April 25, 2018, on Bravo.

4. *Ferris Bueller's Day Off*, directed by John Hughes (Los Angeles: Paramount Pictures, 1986).

5. "Myers-Briggs Type Indicator® (MBTI®)," The Myers-Briggs Company, accessed December 1, 2023, https://www.themyersbriggs.com/en-US/Products-and-Services/Myers-Briggs.

6. Hannah Lack, "Remember when Dolly Parton fully subverted the 'dumb blonde' cliché with her '80s excess styling?" last modified August 5, 2020, https://www.cnn.com/style/article/remember-when-dolly-parton/index.html.

ABOUT THE *Author*

Martina "The Marketing Girl" Barley is the founder and CEO of Uptown Marketing, a digital marketing partner that analyzes market areas, agency structure, production goals, and much more to develop personalized campaigns for insurance agents. Born out of Martina's intuition and fearless decision-making, Uptown has grown into an industry-leading, seven-figure company with 12 dedicated team members, all of whom never hesitate to make big, bold moves if it means helping agents stand out from the competition.

Prior to Uptown Marketing, Martina spent 10 years in insurance, marketing, and sales, breaking records within highly competitive spaces and generating millions of dollars in revenue. She is the only one at her former company to ever generate more than $1 million a year in new business sales. She has been featured in several publications, including *CanvasRebel Magazine*, *Voyage Dallas*, *Shoutout DFW*, and *Bold Journey*, and has appeared on many insurance industry podcasts. Her company's podcast, *The Uptown Girls Podcast*, launched in 2023 and explores the genuine challenges of entrepreneurship: building relationships, leading teams, and all things sales and marketing.

Martina has a passion for real estate and owns Airbnb and rental properties through her company, Martina Nicole Properties LLC. She also dedicates time and resources to Girls on the Run of Greater Rochester, an organization close to her heart.

Martina received her BA in communication and media studies from the State University of New York Brockport. She holds an Advanced Digital Marketing Certification from Cornell University as well as a Google Ads Certification. She lives with her husband, stepsons, and two goldendoodles in her hometown of Rochester, New York. She's happiest in a great outfit with a cold glass of rosè, surrounded by friends and family.

Made in the USA
Monee, IL
09 February 2024